THE CHILDREN OF TOMORROW

Om Swami is a mystic who lives in the Himalayan foothills. Prior to renunciation, he founded and ran a multi-million dollar software company with offices across the world. He is also the author of the bestselling books *If Truth be Told: A Monk's Memoir* (HarperCollins, 2014), *The Wellness Sense: A Practical Guide to Your Physical and Emotional Health Based on Ayurvedic and Yogic Wisdom* (HarperCollins, 2015), *When All Is Not Well: Depression, Sadness and Healing – A Yogic Perspective* (HarperCollins, 2016), *The Last Gambit* (HarperCollins, 2017), and *Mind Full to Mindful: Zen Wisdom from a Monk's Bowl* (HarperCollins, 2018).

D0925692

Also by Om Swami

Plus, nuggets of wisdom and humour served twice a month on www.omswami.com

THE CHILDREN OF TOMORROW

A MONK'S GUIDE TO MINDFUL PARENTING

OM SWAMI

HarperCollins *Publishers* India

First published in India by
HarperCollins *Publishers* in 2019
A-75, Sector 57, Noida, Uttar Pradesh 201301, India
www.harpercollins.co.in

2 4 6 8 10 9 7 5 3 1

P-ISBN: 978-93-5302-934-0
E-ISBN: 978-93-5302-935-7

www.omswami.com

Typeset in 10.5/14 Palatino Linotype
Manipal Digital Systems, Manipal

Printed and bound at
Thomson Press (India) Ltd

MIX
Paper
FSC FSC® C010615

This book is produced from independently certified FSC® paper to
ensure responsible forest management.

CONTENTS

CONTENTS

Nurture

My Thoughts On…

WHY THIS BOOK?

In a quaint country town lived a pastor well known for his insights on parenting. People travelled far and wide to seek his counsel. It was said that this young pastor had condensed all the great learnings of parenting into ten simple instructions which he called 'The Ten Commandments of Parenting'. He proudly displayed them right at the church's entrance. Parents, be it aspiring, experienced or new, devoured his instructions and lived by them. When the pastor turned thirty-five, he married a demure young woman from his congregation.

Two years later, they had their first child; a chubby cheeked daughter they lovingly named Mary. That the pastor would turn out to be a great father (no pun intended) was a given. After all, he was the original author of the ten commandments of parenting. Soon, the pastor discovered that sometimes he had to make certain exceptions to his own commandments for his little daughter – although a bundle of joy, she was also a little tyke who drove him up the wall at the drop of a hat. One night, as he sat exhausted by his daughter's bedside, he had a sudden realization. The next morning, he ran to the church and renamed the title of the ten commandments. Up went the new header that now read:

'Ten Laws of Parenting'

Three years after the birth of his daughter, the pastor's wife gave birth to a healthy son whom they named George. Now the pastor was juggling his job, family, social and religious duties. A bald patch had already begun to peek out from under the shiny, blond hair he once had. After being a parent for just four years, he had another epiphany and decided to change the title of his commandments again. This time, the sign 'Ten Laws of Parenting' was replaced with:

'Ten Rules of Parenting'

Some more time passed and they had one more child, another daughter, Lara. Seven years, three children and several parent-teacher association (PTA) meets later, the pastor figured that he had, in fact, been a fool! There were no rules when it came to parenting. Once again, he printed a new header to replace the old one and pasted it outside the church. But this time he placed it discreetly, near the community board.

'Ten Guidelines of Parenting'

A mere one year later, his wife was pregnant again and gave birth to their second son, Gregory. With a screaming and kicking Mary, George, Lara and now Gregory in tow, the pastor set out to attend Sunday Church. Before addressing his congregation that morning, the pastor handed a new title to the administration clerk and asked that it be pasted on the back door of his church.

'Ten Tentative Ideas on Parenting,' it read.

So is this book. In a way.

There are no hard or fast rules when it comes to parenting; no clear dos and don'ts, no absolute rights or wrongs. Everything is relative, subjective and circumstantial. Any evidence of great parenting is mostly anecdotal at best.

Every year, I meet a few thousand people in small groups. Out of these, at least two thousand or so I meet one-on-one including a few hundred children, from ages five to grown-ups well into their mid- to late twenties.

'I don't know what to do with my mother,' said a young boy to me, 'and she doesn't know what to do with me. I don't know what the solution is.'

'We have no communication in the family,' a lady said to me once. 'If I enter my children's room, they instantly ask, "What do you want?"'

'My parents just don't understand me,' said a fourteen-year-old girl to me the other day. 'The whole world thinks they are very nice people, whereas in reality they are very nasty. They argue and fight all the time. I hate going back home after school.'

'My son says, "Your position means nothing,"' a very prominent politician said to me once. 'If you look at how big the world is, no one knows you outside your constituency.'

'And what does your son do?' I asked this person.

'He's thirty years old and does nothing,' came the dejected reply. 'He plays video games most of the time and sleeps the rest.'

This is a common scenario in most households. Parents are fed up of their children and children are disgusted with their parents. Many kids admit that they really want to make their parents proud but are helpless in front of the distractions of TV, social media and peer pressure. Others say that no matter what they do, their parents just can't be made happy.

Parents too have similar stories about their children. That their children are very lucky compared to them because when they were growing up, their parents used to beat them senseless. Some say that they have always supported their children and yet the children don't seem to care. Many contend that their son or daughter is so intelligent, it's just that he or she doesn't work hard. And so on.

Over the years, I've had the chance to observe from close quarters as well as track the progress of certain children. It has led me to make certain important discoveries that, given the right guidance at the right time, any child can be made to realize their true potential. While there are no commandments or laws of parenting, the truth is that there are certain spiritual insights I can share with you based on my own knowledge gleaned from experience and various psychological studies. Hopefully, they can help you steer your child in the right direction.

Since the time I can remember, I've lived a life of discipline, believing in the power of knowledge and hard work. Today, the sole purpose of my life is to give my two cents' worth to raise the happiness quotient of our beautiful world by nurturing more happy individuals. Now, as I inch towards the twilight at dusk, I realize more than ever that the future of our world rests on the twilight at dawn: our children. On their tender shoulders rests a great nation, a baffling world and a beautiful planet. It is, therefore, my dharma to share what little I know so that a parent's hand is raised to protect a child and not abuse them. Let's strive to create an environment where the billion possibilities in their impressionable brains are given the opportunity to be realized. For a moment, envision them walking in a world (created by us adults) with their heads held high, with hope in their hearts, and a spark in their eyes.

Walk with me.

Dad: You'll never amount to anything because
you procrastinate.
Son: Oh, yeah? Just you wait!

MAKING A GENIUS

In 1973, four-year-old Susan opened the cupboard of the guest room in her house and saw many chess pieces fall out of a small bag. Just next to them was a rolled-up chess mat. She took the mat out and looked at the pieces with the kind of intrigue comparable to any other child of her age.

'What are these, Mummy?' Susan asked innocently, holding a piece in her hand and examining it.

'These are chess pieces, Zsuzsa,' she said, careful to not sound too enthusiastic, worried it might kill Susan's excitement. When parents are too excited to introduce something to a child, the child almost always rejects it. I don't think children do it consciously – it's more a reflex action in the beginning. They hear parents saying *no* all the time and that *no* becomes their standard response too. And once children discover the joys of rebellion, they stick with their original 'no' for a long time. Klara Polgar, however, was better prepared.

Eight years earlier, in 1965, Laszlo Polgar, a teacher in Hungary, had started courting Klara by writing letters. He held two degrees in psychology and education and a PhD with his dissertation in developmental capabilities. In his spare time, he would play chess. During their courtship, Laszlo had told Klara that he was working on a lifelong experiment of making geniuses and that he 'needed a wife to jump on board'. Klara too held three degrees and spoke eight languages. She wanted to marry someone who could match her intelligence. She liked Laszlo's research, hypothesis, and his personality, of course, and the two got married. From USSR, she moved to Hungary to be with Laszlo and they started out in a modest apartment in Budapest.

In 1969, their first daughter, Zsuzsanna – also known as Zsuzsa, whose Western name was Susan Polgar – was born. Numerous times the two parents had reiterated their commitment to each other that the idea was not just to make a genius but rather a 'happy genius'. While attainment in life is important, a sense of fulfilment is even more important. When you feel you are progressing in your desired area, you experience greater fulfilment and this in turn helps you remain happy and motivated.

The moment to put the hypothesis to test had arrived with Susan's fascination towards the chess pieces. This was the beginning of a lifelong and insightful experiment. It might appear a matter of chance that Susan discovered the chess pieces but in reality, it was anything but that. Klara and Laszlo had planned much before their daughter's birth that they would carry out the chess experiment so that it would be easier to measure brainpower.

Klara Polgar opened up the chess mat and showed her four-year-old daughter how the pieces moved. She was careful not to sound too excited or make Susan feel that she should be playing chess because her parents wanted her to. Instead, she kept it low-key and fun. You can get anything done by anyone if you can make them think it's their idea. In other words, when people, particularly children, feel that it's their decision to do something, they will find the motivation to take it up and persist even in the face of challenges.

In the evening when Laszlo returned home, Klara shared how Susan showed interest in chess. The parents sat down, set up their chess set, and began playing a game. As children usually do when parents seem to be enjoying an activity, Susan – who was frolicking around until now – came and settled near the board. She began asking questions, hovering around her parents, and was beginning to get more and more fascinated with the chess pieces. They were careful not to ask her to observe their game or to play or learn it. They just played and enjoyed themselves (or at least pretended to enjoy).

In the years that followed, with great patience, persistence and dogged-determination, Laszlo began training Susan. The journey proved particularly hard. Not because Susan didn't want to play chess or Laszlo wasn't equipped to teach her, it's just that chess was entirely a male-dominated sport at the time. Laszlo and Klara, however, knew that their daughter could play as good as anybody else, male or female.

Often, when Laszlo would take Susan to chess clubs, other players at the club would think that it was Laszlo who had come for a game and had simply brought his daughter along. They thought he was crazy for wasting his time teaching chess to his daughter. And when a seven or eight-year-old Susan would beat seasoned players, many would usually either refuse to shake hands in the end or make excuses like, 'I am sick', 'I have a headache', 'I didn't sleep last night' and so on. This didn't deter the father-daughter duo. On the contrary, it only strengthened their resolve to prove to the world that girls were equally good, if not better than boys.

Laszlo and Klara continued Susan's intensive and specialized training. Meanwhile, they became parents to two more daughters – Sofia Polgar in 1974 and Judit Polgar in 1976. Against all odds, they applied the same principles of parenting and training on Sofia and Judit. The result, you ask? Let me state it out one by one:

Susan Polgar won her first Under-11 chess tournament at age four. At twelve, she won the World (Girls) Under-16 championship. At fifteen, she became the top-rated female chess player in the world. Going through the conventional Grandmaster (GM) norms applicable to men, she became a chess grandmaster at the age of twenty-two. In 1996, twenty-seven-year-old Susan Polgar was crowned the women's chess champion.

While raising Susan, her parents had learnt more about parenting and intensive training, which meant that they could provide an even better environment and coaching to their second daughter Sofia who, at the age of eleven, became a world Under-14 girls chess champion.

Armed with more experience and insight, it was only natural that their youngest daughter, Judit, was brought up in the most conducive environment for the making of a genius. Her siblings played chess which meant that the game was all they mostly talked about, at the dinner table. Her parents no longer had the over-cautiousness and anxiety most parents have with their first child. Their parenting skills were sharpened by now; they could maintain a better balance between giving personal freedom to their child and living up to a certain level of discipline. As a result, Judit's accomplishments exceeded her parents' expectations.

At age twelve, Judit Polgar had thirty-five more points in FIDE rating (world chess rating) than the erstwhile world women chess champion. At age fifteen, she became the youngest chess grandmaster, far ahead of any male chess grandmaster throughout the history of the game. Judit is generally considered the strongest female chess player of all time. At age ten, she not only took on chess grandmaster Lev Gutman, but also won against him.

At age five, Judit defeated a family friend without even looking at the board.

'You are good at chess,' the friend joked after the game, 'but I'm a good cook.'

'Yeah?' Judit said, without batting an eyelid. 'So do you cook without looking at the stove?'

All three daughters were home-schooled by Klara with a specialization in chess. They figured a long time ago – as an increasing number of parents are discovering today – that there was little sense in sending their children to a traditional school where regard for individual growth and understanding the temperament of each child was negligible. By the time most children come back home from school in the afternoon, they are tired and a whole day seems gone. To expect that they would then pursue intensive training in anything else at all is neither practical nor reasonable.

According to the eldest sister Susan, Judit was a slow-starter but very hard working. Laszlo too said that a happy genius is the sum of labour + luck + love + freedom. He studied intelligence when he was a university student and later recalled: 'When I looked at the life stories of geniuses, I found the same thing ... They all started at a very young age and studied intensively.' Before even becoming a father, he had studied the biographies of four hundred people right from Socrates to Einstein and everyone in between and discovered the same pattern over and over again.[1] 'The experiment is not finished yet,' says Laszlo Polgar. 'It began twenty-three years ago with a simple premise: that any child has the innate capacity to become a genius in any chosen field, as long as education starts before their third birthday and they begin to specialize at six.'[2]

In my view too, the gist of scores of studies in child and human psychology spanning over several decades is as follows:

1. Every child is a promise.[3]
2. That promise can be turned into a genius.
3. Such a genius can be a happy person.
4. Coaching begins when children are very young.
5. It must be fun and playful.

By no means am I suggesting that every parent should try to make a genius out of their child, whether in sports, arts, science or any other field. Nor am I saying that geniuses make this world a better place or that you have to be a genius in life to be happy. As a parent, what path you choose for your child or they choose for themselves and you just support them is your personal matter. It is between you and your child and certainly isn't my prerogative. Not even for a moment am I saying that every child should be pushed to their limits and not allowed to lead an easy life. On the contrary, I believe there's little sense in taking away a child's personal freedom by pushing them to do something they don't want to. Such a tug-of-war between parents and children turns toxic very quickly.

Irrespective of what you and I think, the truth is that your child carries a seed of greatness. They represent an opportunity to explore the immense human potential. You can help them make a difference to our world, to be the best in whatever they undertake. As a parent, you *can* make them aware of that possibility in a way they will understand, and help them walk the path they wish to pursue.

In the following chapters, I share how to go about building character in a child's mind so they are able to weather every storm with grace and yet, continue to sail through. Every daughter is a Gandhi, an Einstein or a Mozart waiting to be discovered. Every child has the potential to become a Picasso, a Ronaldo or a Nelson Mandela. Not everything is in our control but with a great deal of what is, you *can* as a parent vastly increase the chances of ensuring your child reaches the heights of greatness without being pushy or preachy.

It begins with instilling a sense of excellence in all aspects of life, an exercise which is a lifelong journey.

"NOW THAT YOU'RE 10, WE CAN TELL YOU
THE TRUTH: BEAUTY ISN'T ACTUALLY
IN THE EYE OF THE BEHOLDER,
THERE ARE INTERNATIONAL STANDARDS...
AND YOU HAVEN'T MET THEM."

THE WORD 'PARENT'

Denmark has been rated one of the happiest countries in the world every year since 1973. That's forty-five years in a row. I have worked with Danes in the past and was surprised by the ease of doing business with them. There was a sense of professionalism as well as a casualness that they radiated. My first Danish client, an executive in a billion-dollar firm, who was in Oslo at the time, even took me around sightseeing on my first visit, thinking I might get bored in my hotel room in the evening. I never had that courtesy extended to me by any client in any other part of the world, nor was this something I ever did for my vendors. It was a weekday and yet there was not a sign of stress in his speech or actions. How to handle life is something we all learn quite early on.

I thought: the Danes have got to be doing something right. What do they know that we don't? As a nation, even with all the religion, gurus and spirituality, we can't claim to have happier individuals as compared to other nations. With this in mind, I began my research and came across a ton of inspiring literature. Recently, I read a wonderful little book by Meik Wiking that talked about the Danish way of life. Called *The Little Book of Hygge*, it read:

Hooga? Hhyooguh? Heurgh? It is not important how you choose to pronounce or even spell 'hygge'. To paraphrase one of the greatest philosophers of our time – Winnie-the-Pooh – when asked how to spell a certain emotion, 'You don't spell it, you feel it.'

However, spelling and pronouncing 'hygge' is the easy part. Explaining exactly what it is, that's the tricky part. Hygge has been called everything from 'the art of creating intimacy', 'cosiness of the soul' and 'the absence of annoyance' to 'taking pleasure from the presence of soothing things', 'cosy togetherness' and, my personal favorite, 'cocoa by candlelight'.

Hygge is about an atmosphere and an experience, rather than about things. It's about being with the people we love. A feeling of home. A feeling that we are safe, that we are shielded from the world and allow ourselves to let our guard down. You may be having an endless conversation about the small or big things in life – or just be comfortable in each other's silent company – or simply just be by yourself enjoying a cup of tea.

One December just before Christmas, I was spending the weekend with some friends at an old cabin. The shortest day of the year was brightened by the blanket of snow covering the surrounding landscape. When the sun set, around four in the afternoon, we would not see it again for seventeen hours, and we headed inside to get the fire going.

> *We were all tired after hiking and were half asleep,*
> *sitting in a semicircle around the fireplace in the cabin,*
> *wearing big jumpers and woolen socks. The only sounds*
> *you could hear were the stew boiling, the sparks from*
> *the fireplace and someone having a sip of their mulled*
> *wine. Then one of my friends broke the silence.*
>
> *'Could this be any more hygge?' he asked rhetorically.*
> *'Yes,' one of the girls said after a moment. 'If there was*
> *a storm raging outside.'*
>
> *We all nodded.*[4]

This is what a good family is about: a sense of warmth and coziness even when storms are raging outside. Anyone who has experienced even a little bit of life (which all of us have, I suppose), know for a fact that storms will rage. And in such situations, you just need something to hold on to, a shelter. Essentially, that's what a family is for; a place where we are surrounded by people we can trust, those who will forgive us for our mistakes and whom we won't hesitate to forgive. Without that love and togetherness, a family is not really a family but just a bunch of frustrated people living under the same roof only because their circumstances require them to.

Good families begin with great parenting. Continuing my research, I felt I should read up on Danish parenting. I'm not suggesting that Danish children don't get stressed or that Indian parents aren't as good. It's just that on multiple occasions, I found that Danes seem to handle stress better than people of other nationalities. They got the job done and yet there was a certain ease about it. No wonder then that I came across a beautiful definition of the word 'parent' in a Danish book on the subject.[5] Turning 'parent' into an acronym, it said the word is a reminder that:

P: P is for Play

A: A is for Authenticity

R: R is for Reframing

E: E is for Empathy

N: N is for No Ultimatums

T: T is for Togetherness and Hygge

Play

> *Free play teaches children to be less anxious. It teaches them resilience. And resilience has proven to be one of the most important factors in predicting success as an adult ... As they say it, if children are always performing in order to obtain something – good grades, awards, or praise from teachers or parents – then they don't get to develop their inner drive. They believe that children fundamentally need space and trust to allow them to master things by themselves, to make and solve their own problems. This creates genuine self-esteem and self-reliance because it comes from the child's own internal cheerleader, not from someone else.*[6]

Whether they play with cars and dolls or video games, one thing that is proven beyond doubt is that making any act of education playful is the easiest way to make it interesting. And when something is interesting to someone, you will have their complete attention. An attentive mind soaks learning and lessons like a sponge absorbs water.

Our current system of education reflects an industrial thinking that might have been useful at a certain point in history but no longer serves its true purpose today. If you are keen on developing your child's talents, you should seriously consider the prospect of homeschooling them. Going to school, if I may put it bluntly, is a sheer waste of time. When a child spends her whole day in school, she's left with little energy or time to do anything else that matters. Our current method of teaching children and making them compete can only train them to lead mediocre lives.

Finland, for one, has completely done away with schoolbooks and taken on an entirely different approach to schooling. You don't need to know trigonometry or calculus if you wish to run a café, for example. You don't have to cram Newton's Laws of Physics if your heart is set on becoming a musician or a painter. In schools and colleges, we spend nearly two decades of our lives learning things that have little bearing on what we may actually do for a living. All that stress from the start itself is mostly unnecessary.

William Doyle, an American teaching in Finland, wrote, 'In Finland, children don't receive formal academic training until the age of seven. Until then, many are in daycare and learn through play, songs, games and conversation. Most children walk or bike to school, even the youngest. School hours are short and homework is generally light … school children have a mandatory fifteen-minute outdoor free-play break every hour of every day. Fresh air, nature and regular physical activity breaks are considered engines of learning. According to one Finnish maxim, there is no bad weather. Only inadequate clothing[7].

Authenticity

Emotional honesty, not perfection, is what children truly need from their parents ... Focusing on the task, rather than over-complimenting the child, is a much more Danish approach. This helps to focus on the work involved, but it also teaches humility. Helping children build on the feeling of being able to master a skill rather than already being a master provides a more solid foundation to stand on and grow from. This promotes inner strength and resilience.[8]

We often shun negative emotions; we rush to our children the moment they are angry, sad or down. This does not leave them with any time for self-contemplation and reflection. A far more powerful option is to speak to them about their emotions; ask them what they are feeling and why they are feeling that way. It's infinitely more effective if we simply ask questions and let them answer rather than tell them what they can or can't feel because the question-and-answer approach makes them think.

Let children know that it's okay to feel angry, jealous, sad and so on. It's more important to help them build an awareness around their feelings rather than reprimand or commend them for what they feel. This is true for a parent too. If you are down or depressed, you can let your child know why you may not be in the best of spirits. If you can share with them why you are feeling that way, it'll help you even more.

Reframing

You see, the way we view life and filter our day-to-day experiences affects the way we feel in general. Many of us are unaware that how we see things is an unconscious choice. We feel that our perception of life is the truth. It's our truth. We don't think of our perception as a learnt way of seeing things (often picked up from our parents and our culture). We see it as just the way things are. This set way of 'the way things are' is called a 'frame', and this frame through which we see the world is our perception. And what we perceive as the truth feels like the truth.[9]

Reframing is a way of approaching the truth differently, helping you take your lenses off, the ones through which you filter the whole world, only seeing what you want to see or how you want to see it. I first studied the concept of reframing almost eighteen years ago during my MBA. At that time, it was purely in the context of corporate strategy and management. It didn't even occur to me back then that it could apply to so many other walks of life.

I remember when we were growing up, a famous saint was charged with financial and sexual crimes. There was a lot of negative press about him and he was being featured on television. My brother and I saw him and began criticizing him.

'This is not nice,' my mother said, hearing our conversation. 'We don't even know the person, we haven't met him, so why badmouth him and infuse negativity in your own mind? If we have nothing nice to say about him, we can at least not speak ill of him.'

For some reason, this lesson has always stayed with me. This was just a way of reframing, of seeing the truth differently. Research shows that parents who help their children see the good in others help them become more positive, kind and forgiving. The important thing to remember, however, is that the best way to teach anything is to do it yourself. Children observe and follow way more than they listen on being told what to follow.

If parents are speaking politely to a waiter, for example, and use 'thank you' and 'sorry' often, children will automatically pick up those habits. If you can use humour, that's even better. The moment you infuse fun in any kind of learning, children open up immediately.

Empathy

Empathy sits in the brain's limbic system. This controls memory, emotions and instinct. It is a complicated neurological system involving mirror neurons and the insula. What many don't realize is that we are biologically predisposed to connect to others. This is made possible through many neuronal systems that are embedded in the right hemisphere of the brain, the mirror neurons being an important aspect of this. The self is not an individual entity, you see, but a relational construct. [In other words], we are all wired for empathy.[10]

Sympathy is 'I feel sorry for you'. Empathy is 'I know how you feel'. Sympathy is closer to pity whereas empathy is a matter of understanding. Empathy, in other words, is to be a sensitive and active listener. And to be just that: a listener. Resist the urge to say things like 'I told you so', 'But you could have done this', or 'This is nothing compared to what I or someone else went through'. Don't offer any advice. Empathy is allowing the other person a space where they can speak without being judged. It's lending them an ear, one that will listen without them having to listen back. Empathy equals open ears and a shut mouth.

Out of care, love and attachment for their children, it is usually very hard for parents to show empathy because their first natural reaction is to offer advice and then somehow pacify the child with more words. This does *not* work. They don't want your opinion at that time; they want to be heard.

So, try and do just that. Hear them out. Let it be for a while. Don't offer any suggestions or opinions unless they ask for it. And when they do, try and be brief. Keep your focus on the matter at hand when you speak and not bring all their past actions and intentions into the picture.

Empathy will strengthen your bond with your child faster than any other emotion.

No Ultimatums

Know the difference between the battles and the war and don't take every battle. Is it really important that their clothes or hair look perfect all the time? Is it really important that they don't wear that Batman shirt one more day? Is it really important that they clean their plate right now because you said so? Or they try spinach because they need to right now? Is it really worth it? This is what you have to decipher and decide with your partner when the big lines need to be enforced ... you have to be consistent, but you don't have to raise soldiers. Remember, kids go through phases in which they don't want to do/eat/wear/say certain things. They grow out of them. If you are consistent with the big lines, they will understand them.[11]

While ultimatums can't be avoided completely, the truth is that they don't really work for the simple reason that parents do give in eventually, and children know it. The child, for example, is aware from the outset that if you are telling him he won't get his video game for a month, chances are that by the time you get to week two, he'd keep on pleading for his game while promising you that he'd listen to you and behave better and so on. And then history would repeat itself. The first time a child is punished is a big thing. Each subsequent punishment becomes less and less effective. I've also seen often that sometimes it no longer remains about the issue or the punishment but a clash of egos. On the one hand is the parent's ego that believes the child ought to listen to him. And on the other is the child's ego that wants some entitlement and say in the matter.

A pertinent question then, is how do you get children to do anything if you can't punish them or give them ultimatums? Clearly, there are moments of disagreement when you as a parent are certain what you want your child to do. The answer lies in building a culture of self-discipline over a period of time in your household. To build such a culture, it is extremely important to involve your children in the rule-making process at a time when they are receptive and all is well. Make reasonable and small goals, and when they are not met, don't give them a big lecture.

The more predictability you build in your model of crime and punishment, so to speak, the more effective your model is going to be. I've elucidated further on the importance of a framework of predictability in a later chapter with the same name. Don't just hand them the rules; involve them in the process.

Togetherness

Feeling connected to others gives meaning and purpose to our lives, and this is why the Danes value hygge so highly. The individual is prized too, but without the interaction and support of others, none of us can be truly happy as a whole person.[12]

Researchers at the Carnegie Mellon University conducted an interesting study that showed how hugs, as a form of social support, protect stressed people from getting sick.[13] Conducted on 404 healthy adults over fourteen consecutive evenings, where some of them received hugs and others didn't, they were subsequently exposed to the common cold virus. Those who had social support or hugs showed less severe illness symptoms.

Like bees are attracted to flowers on their own, children are attracted to playfulness automatically. Togetherness does not mean that we force our children to sit down with us and share everything with us. That is not an action – it's an outcome. There are two aspects of togetherness. First, making it a part of your family's culture, so children know that the whole family will come together to enjoy at least one meal in the day. Second, creating an environment that's conducive to togetherness and shared joy.

Without the second, there won't be a first. For example, if you start lecturing your children when they are having dinner or if they are rebuked or scolded while you are all together, they will soon start avoiding dining with you, and eventually stop spending time with you. It will begin with them leaving the table early before everyone is finished, or by coming late for that dinner. If they don't start feeling the joy, soon they'll make an excuse to not show up at all by staying out, maybe at a friend's on the pretext of some school work, etc. Eventually, they will be bold enough to just stay in their room and close the door (if not lock it from inside). Just remember, this sort of behaviour begins when ultimatums are placed at the wrong time.

If you can get a grip on the four key challenges every parent faces, not only will your relationship with your children reach a whole new wholesome level, you will also help them realize their dreams.

UNDERSTAND

Johny Johny yes papa
Eating sugar no papa
Telling lies no papa
Open your mouth
Ha! Ha! Ha!

LIES
(BREACH OF TRUST)

Mahatma Gandhi's son Manilal Gandhi moved to South Africa to carry on the work his father had left behind – fight against injustice and discrimination. One day, Manilal had a daylong meeting in Johannesburg and he asked his son, Arun Gandhi, to drive him there.

Arun thought this would be a good opportunity to also get his car serviced. They left for the meeting in the morning. In Arun's words:

I dropped my father off for his meeting and got the car to the garage by one. Since it was a long time until five o'clock, I figured I could go to the movies, which I did. That day there was a double feature being shown, and when I got out I checked my watch and realized that it was past five o'clock!

I rushed to the corner where my father had said he would be waiting for me, and when I saw him there, standing in the rain, I tried to think of excuses I could make. I rushed up to him and said, 'Father, you must forgive me. It is taking them longer to repair the automobile than I thought it would take, but if you wait here I will go and get the car. It should be ready by now.'

My father bowed his head and looked downward. He stood for a long moment and then he said, 'When you were not here at our meeting time I called the garage to see why you were late. They told me that the automobile was ready at three o'clock. Now I have to give some thought as to how I have failed, so as to have a son who would lie to his own father. I will have to think about this, so I am going to walk home and use the time during my walk to meditate on this question.'

I followed my elderly father home that rainy, misty night, watching him stagger along the muddy road. I rode behind him with the headlights of the car flashing ahead of his steps. And as I watched him stumbling towards home, I beat on the steering wheel and said over and over, 'I will never lie again! I will never lie again! I will never lie again!'[14]

What struck me as particularly interesting in this story was how Manilal didn't shame his son, he didn't start shouting at him or telling him how Arun had failed him as a son. Instead, he seemed to have understood one thing clearly: children do love their parents. They may act or behave otherwise but deep down they love their parents and need their parents' love and presence in their lives. We can never inspire anyone to do anything by creating fear in their minds or by shaming them. We may force a child – or even an adult – to do something and they may do it well temporarily, but to instill in them a lifelong habit or to inspire them, love remains the only potent weapon. And no, by this I don't mean mollycoddling. I simply mean embracing a sense of acceptance.

Everyone lies. Absolutely everyone on this planet does. Nearly on a daily basis, if not hourly. No one is completely honest despite what they may say or claim. In fact, in an interesting study done in 2002 at MIT, they found that more than 60 per cent of the participants lied an average of three times within the first ten minutes of a conversation. This too when there was no real motivation to lie. They were not being rewarded for lying and yet they did. What's worse is that most of them only realized they were fibbing when videotapes of their conversations were played back to them. Women lied more about their feelings to come across as likeable while men lied about their feelings to portray themselves as more competent.[15]

Whether we tell lies to others or ourselves, we still lie. Therefore, to act or show surprise when a child lies to you as if they have done something so unforgivable is just taking things too seriously, and taking the matter a bit too far. At the opening of this chapter, I cited the famous nursery rhyme 'Johny Johny, yes papa...' Sometimes, that's the approach you have to take as a parent; that is: bring it to the attention of the child that you know they have lied and take it easy from there. You can still convey that lying is not good without interrogating or shaming them. For the longest time, we have regarded truth as a virtue (and it is). Equally bare is the fact that no one is completely truthful. It's like the famous quote, 'A classic is a book that everyone talks about but no one reads.' Truth too is an instruction everyone gives but no one follows.

If I meet one hundred troubled parents in a given month – and I'm being conservative with this figure – at least forty of them complain about their child or children lying to them. The first time parents discover that they are being lied to, it comes as a complete shock to them. And, if psychological evidence is to be believed, children start lying as early as age three. In fact, studies have shown that a four-year-old may lie at least once every two hours and a six-year-old child almost every hour. I read an interesting quote in a wonderful book, *Nurtureshock*, that devoted an entire chapter to why kids lie, complete with contemporary and primary research. It said, 'We may treasure honesty but the research is clear. Most classic strategies to promote truthfulness just encourage kids to be better liars.'

The authors, Po Bonson and Ashley Merryman, cite the research of Dr Victoria Talwar, a leading expert in children's lying behaviours, based out of Montreal. Dr Talwar has run numerous experiments and proved it beyond any doubt that on most occasions, parents can't tell if their kids are telling the truth or not. Children (like adults) are adept in filling in the details that make a lie come alive.[16]

Personally, I've realized that regardless of the circumstances or the nature of lying, it's important to handle such incidents with grace. If you know your child has done something wrong, your manner and tone of questioning will make a huge difference to how much of the truth you are able to extract from them. If we are going to shame a child for lying, such behaviour will not encourage speaking the truth and will only help them in covering up better.

Equally worse is when parents put children on the spot. When you know they have done something wrong, asking them if they indeed did it or forcing them to confess is not the right strategy either. I quote:

> *Talwar says parents often entrap their kids, putting them in positions to lie and testing their honesty unnecessarily. Last week, I put my three-and-a-half-year-old daughter in that exact situation. I noticed she had scribbled on the dining table with a washable marker. With disapproval in my voice, I asked, 'Did you draw on the table, Thia?' In the past, she would have just answered honestly, but my tone gave away that she'd done something wrong. Immediately, I wished I could retract the question and do it over. I should have just reminded her not to write on the table, slipped newspaper under her colouring book, and washed the ink away. Instead, I had done exactly what Dr Talwar had warned against.*
>
> *'No, I didn't,' my daughter said, lying to me for the first time.*
>
> *For that stain, I had only myself to blame.*

If you wish to encourage truth, creating an environment that's conducive to it is non-negotiable. Merely telling the child that they won't be punished for speaking the truth does not cut it. It's important to understand that most kids, as well as adults, lie because they want to avoid conflict, they want to make you happy, they want to be the bearer of good news. If you are going to reward hearing good news as opposed to hearing the truth, their focus will be not on telling you what actually happened but on what they think you want to hear happened.

Going back to the findings of Dr Victoria Talwar, she designed an interesting experiment. In it, one by one, children between the ages of five and seven were asked to sit in a chair facing the wall and the researcher would use a toy that made some noise. If the child could make three right guesses, they would win a prize. The first two would be easy guesses whereas the last one would be entirely unrelated. For example, they would bring a toy duck that quacked and a dog that barked in the first two guesses, whereas in the third, there would be two objects: a soccer ball and a musical greeting card playing some tune. The researcher would then excuse herself and leave the room on some pretext or the other, warning the child to not peek.

Unbeknownst to the child, the researcher would actually wait outside and observe through a camera if they did peek. Most children not only looked, but also lied without batting an eyelid, otherwise how could they guess that a soccer ball made the sound of a piano. They came up with crazy explanations about how they had made that guess. I quote an insightful passage from the book:

> *Lying demands both advanced cognitive development and social skills that honesty simply doesn't require. 'It's a developmental milestone,' Talwar has concluded.*

Indeed, kids who start lying at two or three – or who can control verbal leakage at four or five – do better on other tests of academic prowess. 'Lying is related to intelligence,' confirmed Talwar, 'but you still have to deal with it.'

...

Just removing the threat of punishment is not enough to extract honesty from kids. In yet another variation (of an experiment on lying), Talwar's researchers promise the children, 'I'll not be upset with you if you peeked. It doesn't matter if you did.' Parents try a version of this routinely. But this alone doesn't reduce lying at all. The children are still wary; they don't trust the promise of immunity. They are thinking, 'My parent really wishes I didn't do it in the first place; if I say I didn't, that's my best chance of making my parent happy.'

Meaning, in these decisive moments, they want to know how to get back in your good graces. So it's not enough to say to a six-year-old, 'I will not be upset with you if you peeked, and if you tell the truth you'll be really happy with yourself.' That does reduce lying – quite a bit – but a six-year-old doesn't want to make himself happy. He wants to make the parent happy.

What really works is to tell the child, 'I will not be upset with you if you peeked, and if you tell the truth, I will be really happy.' This is an offer of both immunity and a clear route back to good standing. Talwar explained this latest finding: 'Young kids are lying to make you happy – trying to please you.' So telling kids that the truth will make a parent happy challenges the

kid's original thought that hearing good news – not the
truth – is what will please the parent.

It was May 1986. I was six-and-a-half years old and had just got into the second grade in my school. It was so boring. Each lesson was held by the same teacher in my class. Everyday, for all the subjects, whatever we did in the school, I had to go home and repeat it. This was the homework. Every single day. For example, if I did five sums of math and wrote four sentences in English, I had to go home and rewrite the exact same thing.

I followed it for a couple of weeks before I lost interest. Thinking I was more clever than my teacher, I realized there was no sense in following her instructions. After all, the only difference between what I did in the class versus what I wrote at home was C.W. (classwork) and H.W. (homework). On the left corner of my notebook, if I could change C.W. to H.W., that would become my homework.

After this profound realization, I figured I didn't have to study at home. As soon as I would reach home, I would open my notebook, erase C and write H. Homework done. Whenever my parents enquired if I had finished, I would just nod confidently and flash my notebook. This worked really well for about a month. And then the inevitable happened.

'Submit your notebooks for checking,' my teacher announced to the class.

I tried to avoid it but ours was a small class. I told her that I forgot it at home and that I would bring it the next day. I'd hoped she would forget but she didn't. She asked for my notebook again and I obliged.

'What is this?' she said, flipping through the pages. 'This is all homework. Where is your classwork notebook?'

She thought I might have had two separate notebooks for each.

'I forgot it at home,' I lied. 'I'll bring it tomorrow.'

I went back to my seat, both relieved and scared. The next day, I wasn't sick, it didn't rain buckets, no famous politician was assassinated, my tummy wasn't hurting, my head was fine so I really had no excuse to not go to school. I didn't want to but I had no choice.

'Where's your notebook?' she asked me as soon as the class started.

I dilly-dallied and pretended that I was searching for it in my bag but this time she wasn't having any of it.

'Come right here!' she ordered.

My heart was thumping. I walked up to her slowly and with my head hung low, I kept looking down at the floor. I could see some dust particles on the concrete floor, a tiny piece of chalk that was stuck where two slabs joined.

'Where's your notebook?' she screamed at me. Clearly, she was now frustrated and irritated.

'I don't have it.'

'What do you mean, you don't have it?'

I told her what I had been doing the past month, simply erasing the C of C.W. and replacing it with H. I was in the process of saying sorry, when, bang! she whipped her hand across my face.

My world stood still, the surroundings disappeared.

It was a spectacular strike, a resounding slap that caught me completely off-guard. The left side of my face stung, burnt. I had never been slapped and had no clue that it hurt so much. There was pin drop silence in the class. Standing there, I kept my head down, a feeling of shame smeared my glum face.

No matter how strong or rebellious a child may appear, however well he or she may seem to handle it, the truth is that physical abuse completely destroys self-esteem.

My teacher wrote a long note in my diary saying how I was not only irresponsible and a liar, but that I also cheated and never did my homework. Turning C.W. to H.W. didn't count as homework, apparently! I was asked to get the note signed from my father.

A long day passed and I went home and I pleaded with my mother that if she, instead of my father, could sign the note, it would make things easy. But she politely refused and said that when it came to my education, she would not like to hide the truth from my father. Anything else, she might have considered but not this. 'Simply tell him the whole truth,' my mother encouraged me.

Like a meek calf, I approached my father and shared what had transpired at school. I told him that I had not been doing my homework and that I was sorry about it. I gave him the note to sign.

'Are you really sorry?' he asked, 'You are not just saying it to avoid this talk, right?'

'I am actually sorry,' I murmured.

'Do you promise not to repeat it?' He looked at me kindly, brought me closer to him and caressed my head.

'Yes, papa.'

'I'll sign this time,' he chastised me gently, 'but please never cheat again. If sometimes, you don't feel like doing your homework, it's okay. You just tell me so. Cheating is not an option.'

I nodded. He didn't give me a big lecture or teach me morality. That was the entire conversation.

'If you have a problem, you call me,' my father wrote back to my teacher, 'but you must never touch my child again. You are not to hit him. Ever.'

I went back to school with my head held high. My teacher frowned at the reply, said nothing of it and asked me to go back to my seat. My father's support and words at the time weren't just calming and soothing. In fact, they became the seeds of truth and fearlessness in my life. I figured I could share my thoughts and mistakes with him. Knowing that he would try to understand and not punish me for my errors in judgement and actions became a great pillar of strength.

When we are born, our first ideals are almost always our parents. No doubt that parenting is perhaps the most difficult job in the world. The fact remains that parents' behaviour — towards others, their offspring and each other — is the single most important element that influences the core values in their children. Children observe.

I am not suggesting that parents should treat their children with kid gloves at all times. That can be just as detrimental to a healthy upbringing. You need to be firm when you ought to be. A family where speaking the truth is encouraged, where there is open communication, where children are not lectured for every act that is contrary to a parent's preference, is bound to enjoy great bonding and love. Children brought up in such families will grow up to be confident individuals. Such children will become compassionate adults and perhaps great leaders.

Once a student prepared all night for a zoology test but when he appeared for it in the morning, the teacher had introduced a surprising format for evaluation. There were many cages with birds in them. The enclosures were covered so you could only see the feet of the birds. It was a viva the teacher would do one on one.

'You are to tell me the name of the bird by looking at its feet,' the teacher announced.

The student was mad because he wasn't expecting this at all. He failed the test miserably and quickly made his way to the exit.

'Wait!' the teacher hollered. 'What is your name? I need to mark it.'

'*You* tell me, buddy!' the student turned around, raised his own trousers, and shouted. 'Look at my feet and guess my name!'

I don't think we can entirely blame our children for their lack of interest in studies because our current education system is deeply flawed. It strives to turn you into an average thinker, so you may be useful to an average society. It fosters conformity, not discovery. Your inventions, research and talents must adhere to its standards. More than 80 per cent of the stuff I studied in school I have never utilized in real life. That's a lot of wastage of time and energy. It's no wonder that we are increasingly more restless and distracted than ever before, studying things we don't want to, pursuing careers we don't like, living lives we almost loathe.

Much of this can be avoided if children could get a pat on their backs at the right time, an encouraging word from their teacher, a display of understanding from their parents, a bit of compassion, a little empathy. That's all it takes to transform average minds into extraordinary ones. More than siblings, peers, friends, religion, the two sets of people who make the most difference to a child's life are parents and teachers. So much so that, at times, the roles become interchangeable.

As a parent, sometimes things may become extremely difficult and you may lash out. I don't want you to feel guilty for it. If children can make mistakes, so can parents. Just have a big heart, admit your faults and go back to being loving.

You can't make a point by shouting. Ultimately, love is the only way to transform anyone. You can be firm and yet loving. If you are willing to be loving and patient, children will come around. Such is the power of love. In my view, it is the essence of good parenting and upbringing. No other person can ever fill the shoes of a loving parent.

Love and acceptance alone can foster an environment of trust.

'Mummy,' a young girl said pointing to her mother's head, 'you have some grey hair. Why?'
'Every time you trouble me, daughter,' the mother said, 'I get a grey strand.'
'Oh … now I know why!'
'Know what?'
'That's why your mum's head is full of grey hair!'

ANGER
(WAIT A MINUTE)

❧❦❧

I was about seven or eight years old when this happened. We used to have a lady in our home who would come to do the dishes and clean every morning while my parents were at work. Sometimes, she would come in the afternoon. She was such an integral part of our routine and life that no one in the family thought of her as a helping hand or domestic help but more as a family member. We called her Massi (maternal aunt). She had two sons – the elder one suffered from leprosy but the younger one was fine. He had recently started going to preschool.

My summer vacations had started but his hadn't. One afternoon, Massi brought him to our house and asked me if I could drop him off at their place while she worked in our home. His father would be there, she told me. I was only too eager to take him there. After all, this would give me the opportunity to take my brother's bicycle out for a ride. My own bicycle at the time used to be a small one, not big enough for two people. My brother's was a large-frame bicycle with a bar in front and a carrier at the back.

Fearing that Massi's son might fall – if I let him sit in the back and hold on to my seat while I paddled through bumpy roads – I told him that I would put his schoolbag on my shoulders while he could sit on the bar in front whereby I could monitor him at all times. He was only no more than four years of age and agreed to whatever I said.

So, I parked my bicycle, lifted him and put him on the bar, quickly took his bag and we were on our way. After riding for about a hundred metres, I realized that his feet were hanging in the air while he sat comfortably on the bar clutching the handle of my bicycle. I wouldn't even have noticed if we lost his shoes, I thought. If one of them came undone, the other would also go waste. I certainly wouldn't be able to buy new shoes for him. Working all this out in my head, I decided that it was best if he took off his shoes and I secured them on the carrier behind.

Between the two of us, since I was the elder one taking him home, we concluded that I was indeed the wiser one and that he should just do what I asked him to. He agreed, happily. Once again, we were on our way to his house, now with his shoes secured on the carrier. All through the way, I kept checking to ensure that his shoes were still there. I myself only had one pair of school shoes at home that would get replaced when I outgrew them and for any other issues, they would only be repaired. So, I knew the importance of shiny, new school shoes like his.

We reached his home and I saw his father sitting outside in the verandah. I parked my bicycle and checked again to see if they were there. They were.

I helped the boy get down and he rushed to hug his father who embraced him tightly and made him sit on his lap. I was just behind him, locking my bicycle and carrying his school bag.

'Where are your shoes?' his father asked him, checking his feet to see only socks on. They were still securely fastened on the carrier since I thought I would tell his father that he could take the shoes from my bicycle, and the bag I had brought with me.

The little boy pointed at the bicycle but the father couldn't understand anything.

'Oh that,' I said jokingly, 'we lost them on the way.'

Before I could do anything or say more, even before I could assess what was happening, *phhtaak! phhtaak! phhtaak!* He started slapping his son. Within just a few seconds, he must have slapped him about four times.

'Uncle! Uncle,' I intervened. 'I'm only joking. His shoes are there on my bicycle.' I continued, 'I'm sorry! Please listen. I was only joking! The shoes are safe!'

By the time I finished my sentence, a couple of more slaps had been unleashed on the little one who was now crying uncontrollably. The moment his father realized that all that spanking was for nothing, he stopped. No one knew what to do at that time. He started stroking and caressing his son and telling him that he was sorry. I was telling *both* of them that I was sorry. It was an unnecessary situation to be in and extremely awkward. I felt terrible for being the cause of someone getting a beating because of me. In fact, I felt so bad and awkward that even to this day, more than thirty years later, I still remember this incident vividly.

I remember his navy-blue shorts, his white shirt, his little tie, the metallic dark green colour of my bicycle, the rising mercury in the month of June, the roads, their verandah that did not have tiles like ours but simply mopped with clay and cow dung; none of that is lost on me to this day. I distinctly remember the pain I experienced for creating that entirely unavoidable situation, causing someone grief. That was the last time I ever joked like that. It was a conscious act on my part. I can't call it a genuine mistake even if my intention wasn't for him to get a scolding.

I quickly took leave and quietly rode back. Half an hour had passed by now when I reached home and Massi had left for wherever else she was supposed to go that day.

It was unimaginable for me that a child as tiny and as young as him could get slapped multiple times in a matter of seconds. I mean, not even two seconds before that he was playing in his father's lap and then suddenly I was not only a witness but the cause of that spanking. This is something I have not been able to forgive myself for till date. The point I'm making is that no matter what the circumstances, hitting a child is not going to discipline them.

I know what I'm going to suggest is not easy or practical, but if a parent could wait only a few minutes before showing their first reaction, it would do a whole lot of good to everyone. The blind fit of rage will pass as it always does. When parents hit their child for whatever reason (read: excuse), the child may forget but that does not mean that it did not impact them. The first thing a child experiences when he or she is hit is utter humiliation.

And let me tell you that nothing repairs that humiliation. A child is not going to be okay just because a parent is now showering them with love after calming down. It forever creates a fear in the child's mind. The next time when similar circumstances arise, the child would automatically accept a subservient role. Later in school, university, at work and so on, there's always going to be a side to that child which will surrender to any parental voice. He or she will never know how to respond when faced with authority. I rarely have absolute rules for anything in life but if there is one, then not hitting a child under any circumstances is one of the most important ones.

Daniel J. Siegel and Tina Payne Bryson offer some simple but powerful psychological insights in *No-Drama Discipline*. I quote below a passage highlighting the confusion a child's brain faces when they receive physical punishment.

> *Another important problem with spanking is what happens to the child physiologically and neurologically. The brain interprets pain as a threat. So when a parent inflicts physical pain on a child, that child faces an unsolvable biological paradox. On one hand, we're all born with an instinct to go toward our caregivers for protection when we're hurt or afraid. But when our caregivers are also the source of the pain and fear, when the parent has caused the state of terror inside the child by what he or she has done, it can be very confusing for the child's brain. One circuit drives the child to try to escape the parent who is inflicting pain; another circuit drives the child toward the attachment figure for safety.*

So when the parent is the source of fear or pain, the brain can become disorganized in its functioning, as there is no solution. We call this at the extreme a form of disorganized attachment. The stress hormone cortisol, released with such a disorganized internal state and repeated interpersonal experiences of rage and terror, can lead to long-lasting negative impacts on the brain's development, as cortisol is toxic to the brain and inhibits healthy growth. Harsh and severe punishment can actually lead to significant changes in the brain, such as the death of brain connections and even brain cells.

Another problem with spanking is that it teaches the child that the parent has no effective strategy short of inflicting bodily pain. That's a direct lesson every parent should consider quite deeply: do we want to teach our kids that the way to resolve a conflict is to inflict physical pain, particularly on someone who is defenceless and cannot fight back?[17]

There's no denying that sometimes it's impossible to reason with a child or to make them understand something. I fully accept that children are not always reasonable or accommodating, and it even feels justified to confront them in an abrupt manner or to chastise them. You can be firm with a child and instead say 'No'; you can veto their decisions and demands at times, but it is never advisable to hit a child. If you hit them as a response out of your own frustration, then clearly it's something you as a parent need to fix inside yourself. And if you hit a child in a manner of punishing them, then this will fail to accomplish the desired outcome, if not completely backfire in the future. Whatever behaviour kids observe in their parents, that almost always becomes their own coping mechanism in life. They begin to believe that it's okay to behave and feel that way.

If your objective is to teach a child a lesson, punishing them in an unpredictable manner is certainly not going to achieve that. You may force them to behave in a certain way but that is going to have a temporary effect. The act of disciplining a child is not the same as punishing them. There's a vast difference between the two. In the former you give them a skill, a lesson to be better in the future. In the latter, we merely unload our own frustrations and make them feel bad about an act already done so that they might remember the lesson.

And humiliation is only the first stage after a child is hit. It is then followed by shame and confusion. Each one of us in the divine play of nature is designed to feel strong and empowered. People love it when they feel they are in charge and can make decisions. The sort of freedom you experience with empowerment of the self is indescribable. But the moment a child is hit, an intense feeling of shame overcomes them. Whether or not they think they are at fault is beside the point. A child is not even thinking whether what they did was right or wrong. Shame involves feeling weak and so incapable that one can't even protect themselves. As a species, we are designed to safeguard ourselves. You could be busy doing the most careful task but even a fly coming at a fast speed towards your eye makes you blink. Your subconscious mind knows that you have to blink to protect yourself. It's innate.

However, when a child is hit, even if they can protect themselves, they don't. They know that they can't hit their parent back. This leads to utter confusion in their mind. Can they trust their inner voice which says they can protect themselves but they can't? Can they trust a parent who is supposed to guard them but is attacking instead? Where can they go? Whom can they call? Whom should they listen to?

I meet so many children who have disorders like depression, anxiety, obsessive compulsive disorder (OCD), paranoia, and most of them have either been subjected to or been witness to domestic violence. The helplessness a child feels when hit is very similar to what they experience when parents fight with each other and a child just has to sit and watch it all helplessly.

This doesn't end there. When a child is hit repeatedly, he or she is going to turn rebellious. It's only a matter of time. If they have the opportunity, they'll speak up or move out and if they don't, they'll just stop listening to you. Most people who turn a completely deaf ear to their parents' advice or all things parent-related are usually the ones who were either subjected to spanking or excessive verbal abuse as children. Or, they saw their parents arguing and fighting frequently. Or, they were repeatedly told they were not good enough. In so doing, there comes a moment when the child gives up and begins to believe that they might actually be no good. It is very hard to rescue such a child.

Later they struggle with relationships on all fronts. They may succeed professionally but when it comes to forging lifelong relationships, either at work, home or with friends, they struggle. Either they end up becoming doormats, that is trying to please everyone and constantly looking for approval and appreciation, or they become self-obsessed and fail to see past themselves. Either way, they struggle. This creates havoc in their personal lives once again, repeating history.

A child who is shamed and humiliated either directly with words and actions or indirectly (what they feel when they are being hit), grows into an either a narcissistic person or a very weak one.

So, as a parent, the next time you are really upset and feel that you have no option left other than punishing your child in whichever way you can, just hold on a minute. Let some time pass, even if it's just five minutes. Ask yourself what the objective is behind the punishment you are about to give. Did the child know in advance that their action would attract such a reprimand from you?

Just wait another minute and ask yourself: what was I doing when I was her age?

You may feel that you were very together or a good listener, but if you reflect on it deeply, you'll realize that when we were children ourselves, we made plenty of mistakes too. It's not like we were studying all the time or praying all the time. We may like to believe that we were very good kids, but you and I both know that we messed up in our own ways according to the times we lived in and the opportunities we had.

Hitting a child is not disciplining them – it is but destroying them. I'm sure, as parents, that's not what you ever want for your children.

All women become like their mothers. That is their tragedy.
No man does, and that is his.[18]

DEMANDS
(LIVE WITHIN YOUR
MEANS)

~≈⊘⊱~

Many parents I meet, particularly in India, are saddled with debt. Personal debt is an increasing global phenomenon where more and more people have bigger mortgages, car loans, personal loans and many other kinds of borrowing. What strikes me particularly odd is when parents feel shy to let their children know that they can't afford something. Instead of building that bond in a family where members can speak freely to each other, parents continue to take such pressure on themselves to meet the expectations of their children. It may be hard to digest but I've seen mothers selling their jewellery to buy the latest video game or iPhone for their children. Frequently, parents take out loans to fund the wedding party. For what? For whom? I always wonder. Taking a loan out for education is still not outside the purview of common sense but to borrow money so we may have a grand party to impress those who don't matter is something I fail to find wisdom in.

I already feel the generation gap when I say that many people of my age today were brought up differently. Maybe my thinking is too old-fashioned, but at least everyone slept in peace and woke up happy because there was no burden of any debt.

Both my parents worked for the state government, the electricity board to be precise. As a result, both would get many units of electricity free per month and any subsequent consumption at subsidized rates. Throughout my childhood in the early '90s, our bi-monthly average phone bill was around Rs 7, and sometimes going up to Rs 20. Most of the time it was just the minimum rental payable while our consumption of electricity was in the negative. This was when others in the neighborhood paid anywhere between Rs 50 to Rs 500 as their bill. We were not allowed to frolic in running water or leave a light bulb on when not in use.

'We live in a country, children,' my father would often say to us, 'where millions don't get clean drinking water, they live without electricity. Our state buys electricity from other states. Wastage of natural resources goes against the interest of our nation. It's a crime.'

We were not allowed to let the tap run while we brushed our teeth, for example. 'Use whatever you need to but you must do so diligently' was the mantra. 'Put less in your plate and you can always take another serving. But don't waste food,' he would say. He was very open about how much my mother and he earned. It was a fixed salary, so the amount would be exactly the same every month except near Diwali when they were given bonuses.

When we wanted things like new toys, games, bicycles or in later years, bikes and so on, he would tell us that he would have to save first, particularly if what we wanted was worth more than a few hundred rupees. Although he would hand his entire salary to my mother every month as she could handle any amount of stress with a calm mind, most financial decisions were taken jointly between the two.

I remember when my elder brother, Rajan, took up Commerce in Grade 11, he was quite excited about – and very good at – learning accounting.

'I am sure I can manage your money better,' he said to my father.

'How?'

'I can help you save more.'

My father showed keen interest in this proposition and my parents decided to hand over their salaries to my brother who was seventeen years old at the time. Up till that point our lifestyle entailed the following:

One dinner out every month with the entire family.

Two kilograms of fruits were purchased every second day.

Once a week, they would buy sweetmeats or hot samosas while returning from work and the whole family would eat them together.

Every alternate weekend, we used to have Sunday breakfast outside, which was usually chana-bhaturas and the like, or instead of going out, mother would make a nice breakfast at home. My father too offered to make something nice at times but there weren't many takers in the family!

150 rupees pocket money for my sister, 75 rupees for Rajan and 50 rupees for me.

My sister used to paint, so her monthly tuition fee and cost of canvas, colours, etc., was another Rs 800 to Rs 1000.

The moment Rajan got hold of the money, he made a table estimating every expense and meticulously maintained a ledger. In the true spirit of any accountant, he cut down on the expenses.

'Only 500 for your painting and other hobbies,' he said to my sister. She tried to reason that fine arts was not a hobby for her but her major in her bachelor's degree since she was doing a BA in Fine Arts and Psychology. But Rajan had made up his mind. 'And your, pocket money as well will be Rs 100 from now on.'

There was retaliation and my father agreed to support her from his savings but he said he wanted to give Rajan a full and fair chance at managing the finances. Two days later, he asked Rajan for some money for groceries.

'We'll only buy fruit, once a week,' Rajan said. 'And we don't need 4 kilograms of milk everyday. We'll cut it down to two.'

He put a lid on the weekly sweets and samosas and said that would now be once a month only. He took a cut in his own pocket money and offered to slash mine by 50 per cent as well. I wasn't pleased but it didn't really bother me because not only was I earning my own money through astrology, under the current circumstances, I was the only one who was completely financially independent in the family. Thank God, I didn't have a CFO like Rajan to manage my finances.

Throughout the month, whenever anyone asked for any money, like a true accountant, Rajan would successfully make them feel bad and ask them to find ways to do more with less. The month passed slowly and Rajan ended up saving Rs 3,500 whereas earlier we couldn't save more than Rs 1,500. But this dictatorial rule didn't sit well with Didi and myself – both of us launched a rebellion. Plus, father too believed it was a bit too harsh. Mother was cool, as if she knew from the beginning that this project wasn't going to last.

'You've done great, Rajan,' father said, 'but I need to feed my kids better. You all need to drink milk and eat your fruits. It's not worth it to cut down on these small pleasures of life. You've proved you can save money but saving is not everything, and certainly not at the cost of health and basic necessities in life.'

And so, restoring sanity and world peace, financial control went back to the hands of my mother and life became enchanting and easy once again.

The greatest learning, however, was not that you can always find an avenue to save money no matter what the circumstances. It was something entirely different: a culmination of all that I've shared so far in this chapter. And that is: nothing is more satisfying than to live within your means. Throughout his life, my father never borrowed money. He built one room and my family moved in that house (I wasn't born then). A year later another room was built, followed by yet another, and that's how he built a three-bedroom house. Fourteen years after that, he did an extension and built another room on the top floor. Ten years later, he did another extension and built one more room, now making it a five-bedroom house.

Sometimes we would tell him that he should buy a car as he certainly had the savings. 'I've to save for my daughter's and your education,' he would say. 'I've to save for other emergencies. And my scooter does the job just fine.'

Other times too, if we ever complained of the lack of resources or not having enough, his reply would be a simple one delivered lovingly: 'This is all I can do with what I earn. When you grow up, you are welcome to do more and spend however you like. For now, this is the best I can do.'

It worked. And it's not that I didn't have a video game or a computer, or my brother a Yamaha bike, it's just that everything had to be done within our range of affordability. Buying one bike was good and he could buy two but we were asked to share. We learnt planning and negotiation. At times, one of us would take my father's scooter or simply use the bicycle to get from point A to B. He said buying a second bike was not being extravagant but that he wasn't comfortable using his savings for another one. Those funds would be better utilized on a better education and so on, in his opinion.

It's a habit that was ingrained in our minds too. Borrowing money for a safe investment, like buying a home, is quite different from taking a loan to spend. If you have savings, surely, you are entitled to spend. No doubt, you can use a portion of your savings to treat yourself and your family (and the quantum of such spends is entirely your prerogative). But to borrow money so you may go on a lavish holiday or throw a grand party for your son or daughter's wedding is scarcely wise. It doesn't take an Einstein to know that it's a much better use of your money – hopefully savings and not borrowed – if rather than spending that money on a big wedding, is instead gifted to the newly-wed couple so they may put down the deposit for their own home.

No matter how rebellious or adamant children may seem, if you speak the truth to them, sooner or later, they will understand. Ever so often, I meet parents reeling under children's demands only because children think that their parents are loaded with money whereas they are, in fact, struggling to even pay the next month's car repayment. Sometimes it might be even worse: they don't have money for forthcoming rent or a home loan repayment. Recently, I was telling a young boy to not push his parents to spend too much on his wedding as his parents were going through a financial crunch. 'But my father has money,' the boy said to me. 'He's always giving gifts to our relatives and his friends.' The father, on the other hand, was actually penny-pinching to keep up an all-is-great façade in front of his friends. None of his children knew. I wouldn't either if it were not for his father's confession.

When parents live within their means, children automatically learn the same. And equally important is to have that kind of transparency in your home where your children know the limits of what you can and can't do. As a parent, you must know how much you can spend on what. It is never too early or too late to instil the habit of financial planning and saving in your children.

People who are habitual savers are able to retire early, enjoy more and lead a more secure life. When you know that you are prepared for a rainy day, a fluctuating economy doesn't create anxiety in your heart. But we all know that anxiety is not something we experience just from a volatile stock market or economy but from many other factors too. How should you better prepare yourself and your children for such emotions? The answer is by living the way I've shared so far and by following one simple advice: Show, don't tell.

A small boy was at the zoo with his father. They
were looking at the tigers, and his father was
telling him how ferocious they were.
'Daddy, if the tigers got out and ate you up…'
'Yes, son?' the father asked, ready to console him.
'…which bus would I take home?'

ATTACHMENT
(BUT I NEED YOU)

❧

There was a bird who lived in a nest with his three young chicks. The mother bird had become prey to a vulture and now the male bird protected and reared his offspring till they were ready to fly. One day, he overheard a conversation in a group of woodcutters that they would start felling trees from the next day.

'I must shift you to the woods at the other side of the river,' he said to his three young children. 'From tomorrow, they'll start chopping the trees and this tree too will be felled any day.'

Working at a frantic pace, he collected twigs, feathers and dry leaves from wherever he could and built his nest on a different tree within a few hours. The next morning, he could hear the sound of the woodcutters sawing trees at a distance. It was only a matter of time before they would cut down this tree too, he figured.

Carefully holding his eldest son in his beak, he took flight to park him in the new nest. While they were flying over the river, the father said, 'My son, do you see how hard I'm working to take care of you? One day, I'll get old too and won't be able to fly or move about as easily or as freely. Will you take care of me the way I'm taking care of you now?'

'Of course, father,' the son said, 'I'll do anything for you. I'll even die for you. I'll take care of you till my last breath.'

'I'm disappointed in you, son,' the father said. 'How can you be sure? You are just saying it to get across because right now you are emotional and you need me.' With the detachment that sometimes birds and animals exhibit, he let go of his son and flew back to the old tree.

Taking his second son across the river, he posed the same question to which he also replied with the same vigour and conviction. 'Why do you even ask?' the son-bird said. 'I'll take care of you more than anyone else in the world.'

'You are just emotional right now,' the father said. 'But you should refrain from making empty promises.' With this, he let go of his second son as well and went back to fetch his third one.

On their way to the new nest, he popped the same question to his last and only son.

'See how hard I'm working for you, son?' he said. 'Do you promise to care for me the way I'm taking care of you?'

'I'm sorry, father,' the young bird replied, 'but how can I possibly make that promise? I don't know where my livelihood will take me. I can't be sure where my family may require me to be. I may be busy in meeting many other demands, maybe of my wife and offspring, so I can't possibly make that promise.'

'I'm very proud of you, son. At least, you speak the truth and that's what I wanted to hear.' He flew quietly thereafter for a few minutes when the silence was broken by the young one.

'But I can certainly promise you one thing, father,' he said, 'I'll take care of *my* children the way you are taking care of me.'

This is the eternal cycle of nature. Your parents took care of you, you took care of your children and they will take this care and love forward. There is no doubt that children too are attached to their parents but usually a child's attachment is different from a parent's.

In this deep attachment with their children, most parents (not all), saddle their offspring with a tremendous burden of expectations. You've to choose a certain career, you can't be friends with so-and-so, you must obey these rules, you can't play this sport, you can't do this, you are not doing that enough, look at this person and look at that person and on and on and on. While I agree that it's not possible to not be attached to your children, and I also accept that when parents give such instructions, they are almost always with good intentions, the fact of the matter is that it's unhealthy for the relationship. Besides, just because you have the right intention does not mean you possess the right skill to ask such a thing of your child.

Recently, on the first day of our Bangalore meditation retreat our AV vendor took a double booking and put an inexperienced person in his place to handle our event. The sound quality was shocking. The competent core team that was handling the event and our army of devoted volunteers sensed that the quality of our PA system could have been better.

'Sorry, Swamiji,' someone came to me afterwards and said. 'We'll ensure this doesn't happen tomorrow.'

'Apology accepted,' I said, 'but unfortunately that's unlikely to fix the problem.'

'I'll personally man the PA system tomorrow,' another pitched in.

'I appreciate it,' I replied, 'but are you an expert? Please let's aim to get the vendor back in here.'

To their credit, they took control, pulled up the vendor, made some changes and the rest of the programme went off smoothly.

I went on to explain the difference between intention and skill. It is one thing to have the intention to do something right and it is quite another to have the skill to do so. Sometimes you want to help someone or the other person wants to help you. That may all be very good but unless you possess the right skill, intention is not going to amount to much. This gap between intention and skill is why many of us face failures in our endeavours, whether that's in parenting or anything else.

Parenting is a skill too. When you become a parent for the first time, even a seasonal sneeze from your one-year-old can give you an anxiety attack. Whereas, by the time you are taking care of your third child, even if he gobbles down a bowl of Nutties, you are not alarmed the same way. For now, you have been there, done that. I feel that somewhere, you must also believe that parenting is a skill one can acquire and sharpen, otherwise you wouldn't be reading this book. Having said that, even with all the skills in the world, we can't afford to lose sight of the fundamental truth of a parent–child relationship: your children will be attached to their children the way you are attached to them.

Besides, if you look at it honestly, what was your intention when you chose to bring a child into this world? It's unlikely that the intent was to bring a new life and give her so much love and freedom that each moment of her life would be full of bliss and joy. There is no doubt that parents wish all that for their children and a lot more but that's usually not the original intention. If it was, we could easily adopt a child who is in immediate need of our love, attention and care than go through the process of bringing a child into this world. Somewhere, people become parents because they are looking to grow, to pass on their wisdom and wealth, to fill a sort of void in their lives that their parents, friends, partner, job, education and success cannot. Maybe it's the desire to live all over again, to fulfil your dreams through a younger version of you. And I'm not suggesting that fulfilment here means making them pursue your intended path. Instead, I simply mean a deep sense of fulfilment a parent experiences when their child outshines them. Generally, behind conceiving a child is the deep desire to complete one's own life. It could, in many cases, also be due to pressure from the elders in the family. Either way, we bring a child in this world due to our needs or desires. But that's often hard to admit. And because we are not honest with this admission, we fill ourselves with negativity ('My children are thankless') or make the children feel guilty ('You don't see what I'm doing for you'). Alan Watts called it playing games. I quote:

> When a child comes into the world, the parents play an awful game on it. Instead of being honest, they say, 'We've made such great sacrifices for you. Here we are, we've supported you, we've paid for your education, and you're an ungrateful little bastard.' And the child feels terribly guilty because what we do is we build into every human being the idea that existence is guilt.
>
> The existentialists make a big deal out of this, and you watch out for them because they're hoaxers, and they say that guilt is ontological. If you're not feeling guilty you're not human. And that was because papa and mama said, 'Look at all the trouble you've caused us. You shouldn't dare to exist. You have no rights, but maybe we'll give you some, out of the generosity of our hearts, so that you'll be permanently indebted to us.'
>
> And so everybody goes around with that sort of thing in their background, unless they had different kinds of papas and mamas who didn't play that trick on them. But so many papas and mamas do that. And if they don't do it, somebody else does it. Aunty comes around and says, 'You don't realize what your father and mother have done for you. You think, you know, you can just stay around here and goof off! But they've sweat blood to give you your clothes, and food, and so on, and you ought to be grateful for it.'

But that's not the way to make people grateful. They won't be grateful that way. They'll imitate gratefulness. They'll go and put on a big show and say, 'Oh thank you so much! I feel so indebted to you!' And so on, and so forth, and they'll make it look good. But it isn't real. Because, actually, one's father and mother had a great deal of fun bringing you into being – or we hope they did. And they wanted to do that the worst way. They have no reason to complain about all these things, and try and make the children feel guilty.

But, you see, it's an amazing thing in our culture that everyone is afflicted with ontological guilt. For example, if a policeman comes to the door, everybody is instantly frightened; you wonder, 'What on Earth have I done? And there are certain clergy who are absolute experts in making you feel guilty. They're really marvelous. And there are clergy of all kinds, for all classes, and for all levels of intelligence, and they can make you feel real guilty. Only, you have to watch – always – what games people are playing.

Now, you see, the thing is – that really is a puzzle – is that they don't admit they are playing games. And when a person is playing games, and doesn't admit that they are playing games, then you have some kind of a trickster who isn't really being fair to you.[19]

It is true that parents want the best for their children but that does not necessarily mean that what they want is actually best for their kids. We can't inspire them or make them feel grateful by repeatedly telling them how much we are doing for them. It may sound cruel but it's not a big deal if you are doing a lot for your children. Your parents did that to the best of their capacity and potential and now you are doing the same. I don't deny that when you are so invested in a relationship (for example, parent–child), it is only natural that you expect from the other person too. But that still does not give us the right to clip the freedom of the other person or tell them which career they ought to pursue or whom they should marry and so on.

Somewhere, we have to trust nature, have a bit of faith that in this vast creation where billions and billions of lifeforms are thriving, our children too are connected with the same cosmic intelligence and that they would be guided by their own intuition, aptitude, skills and other forces of nature.

BUILD

A young boy lost one of his contact lenses while playing basketball in his
driveway. He looked around a bit, as thoroughly as he could, but the lens was nowhere to be found.

He went inside and apprised his mother who told him that she would search for it herself.

'But mum,' he said, 'I've already looked for it everywhere and it's impossible to find. It's tiny and totally transparent, as you know.'

The mother, however, still went outside to search and returned with the lens in her hand. All in a matter of less than ten minutes.

'Wow!' the boy exclaimed. 'How on earth did you find it?'

'Well, son,' she replied, 'we weren't looking for the same thing. You were searching for a small piece of plastic. I, on the other hand, was looking for $200.'

IDENTITY CAPITAL
(START SOON)

≈⊗≈

No matter how smart one is, we all go through a phase of identity crisis. Life seems to be at a crossroads and we don't know whether we are heading in the right direction. We feel confused about what we ought to be doing, what the purpose of our life is, and so on. In psychology, it is called an identity crisis.

In our retreats and ashram meets, I meet youths all the time who tell me that they are going through some form of identity crisis. In their mid- to late twenties, they are quite confused about where they stand or how they should take their career and life forward. Their parents tell me they are unable to help their children at this stage. I believe them. It's quite simple: if you have not helped your child build an identity capital, they will have nothing to tap into when undergoing an identity crisis.

For example, if you are going through a financial crisis, to overcome it you are going to use your capital, your resources and assets. In the absence of such capital, the options are quite limited. Dealing with an identity crisis is no different. Meg Jay in her wonderful book, *The Defining Decade*, shares a case study of one of her clients, a twenty-something Helen who approached Meg for therapy because she was going through an identity crisis.[20]

Helen had dabbled in many jobs including being a nanny and a photographer, amongst others. She even joined a yoga retreat to awaken her inner self. She seemed to have had a cool and casual lifestyle but by the time she was twenty-seven, many of her friends who once envied her for her coolness now pitied her for her adventures. Helen had started studying for med school but later changed to the arts. The joy of photography was lost too because the income from it wasn't enough to pay her bills and she still depended on her parents to help her out.

She was at the crossroads in life and waiting for some inspiration to dawn so she could know what she was supposed to do with – and in – her life.

> *Now Helen had hoped that the right retreat or the right conversation in therapy or with friends might reveal, once and for all, who she was. Then, she said, she could get started on a life. I told her I wasn't so sure and that an extended period of navel-gazing is usually counterproductive for twenty-somethings.*
>
> *'But this is what I'm supposed to be doing,' Helen said.*
>
> *'What is that?' I asked.*
>
> *'Having my crisis,' she replied.*
>
> *'Says who?' I asked.*

'I don't know. Everybody. Books.'
'I think you are misunderstanding what an identity
crisis is and how you move out of one,' I said.
'Have you ever heard of Erik Erikson?'

Meg shared with Helen the story of the famous developmental psychologist, Erik Erikson who didn't know who his biological father was. Erik's mother's first husband, whose surname (Salomonsen) Erik inherited, it was discovered was not his father. His mother fled from Copenhagen to Germany and married another man. Erik Salomonsen became Erik Homberger. It was later revealed to him that Homberger was not his father either but a stepfather. For the most part of his life, he suffered from identity confusion and crisis until he changed his name to Erik Erikson.[21]

Continuing with the passage from the book:

Helen and I talked about how Erikson went from identity crisis to the Pulitzer Prize. Yes, he travelled around and slept under some bridges. That's half the story. What else did he do? At twenty-five, he taught art and took some education classes. At twenty-six, he started training in psychoanalysis and met some influential people. By thirty, he'd earned his psychoanalytic degree and had begun a career as a teacher, an analyst, a writer, and a theorist. Erikson spent some of his youth having an identity crisis. But along the way he was also earning what sociologists call identity capital.

Identity capital is our collection of personal assets. It is the repertoire of individual resources that we assemble over time. These are the investments we make in ourselves, the things we do well enough, or long enough, that they become a part of who we are. Some identity capital goes on a résumé, such as degrees, jobs, test scores, and clubs. Other identity capital is more personal, such as how we speak, where we are from, how we solve problems, how we look. Identity capital is how we build ourselves—bit by bit, over time. Most important, identity capital is what we bring to the adult marketplace. It is the currency we use to metaphorically purchase jobs and relationships and other things we want.

Twenty-somethings like Helen imagine that crisis is for now and capital is for later when, in fact, crisis and capital can—and should—go together, like they did for Erikson. Researchers who have looked at how people resolve identity crises have found that lives that are all capital and no crisis—all work and no exploration—feel rigid and conventional. On the other hand, more crisis than capital is a problem too. As the concept of identity crisis caught on in the United States, Erikson himself warned against spending too much time in 'disengaged confusion'. He was concerned that too many young people were 'in danger of becoming irrelevant'.

Twenty-somethings who take the time to explore and also have the nerve to make commitments along the way construct stronger identities. They have higher self-esteem and are more persevering and realistic. This path to identity is associated with a host of positive outcomes, including a clearer sense of self, greater life satisfaction, better stress management, stronger reasoning, and resistance to conformity—all the things Helen wanted.

I encouraged Helen to get some capital. I suggested she start by finding work that could go on a résumé.

'This is my chance to have fun,' she resisted. 'To be free before real life sets in.'

'How is this fun? You're seeing me because you are miserable.'

'But I'm free!'

'How are you free? You have free time during the day when mostly everyone you know is working. You're living on the edge of poverty. You can't do anything with that time.'

Helen looked skeptical, as though I were trying to talk her out of her yoga mat and shove a briefcase into her hand.

Tell me a word you don't know. No, I'm not asking that you tell me a word you may not know the meaning of, but a word you may never have heard. It's not possible, right?

If I ask you to express how your day was, what would you say? You might say, it was good, the usual, tiring and so on. If I asked you to write a paragraph on how your day was, you might state all the things you did during the day. And if I requested you to write an essay, you would have to think a bit more. At any rate, one thing is certain: you will only use the words you know. How much of what you express will be limited to your vocabulary. If you don't know the word 'supercalifragilisticexpialidocious', you won't use that to describe 'something extraordinarily wonderful', for example.

Similarly, we only deal with life based on the things we know. What we know and what we have worked towards (in other words, our skills and talents) create our identity capital. It helps us handle life better. If I don't know something even exists, how would I ever put it to use? What I mean is: when children are growing up, somewhere it's a parents' job to at least make their children aware of the possibilities they have in life. No, that's not done by giving them big lectures but by exposing them to a certain discipline of learning and life; be it a sport, a creative activity or anything else early on in life. To wait till they are ten or eleven is already too late. As Laszlo Polgar contended, we must start early.

It's important to keep in mind that we can never force children to live life a certain way. Yes, at times, we do pressurize them into doing something but it won't last forever. The good news is that it doesn't have to last a lifetime but simply needs to be followed till it becomes their habit. And to make them follow something, you simply need to negotiate it effectively.

"No, Danny can't come out and play. Danny's on death row."

A SENSE OF REALITY
(LET THEM EARN)

✦⚬✦

In 2001, when I started pursuing my MBA at the University of Technology, Sydney, I met a bright fellow who I became good friends with. Let's call him Joshil. We were majoring in different fields but some of our core subjects were the same. It turned out that he was the only son of a big industrialist in India, a US dollar billionaire. At the time, I'd just started my own software company and my annual revenues were just around $500,000. A few months earlier, I had read *Rich Dad Poor Dad* by Robert Kiyosaki which had made it to bestseller charts worldwide.

Joshil was certainly the son of just about as rich a dad as one could imagine and he treated money differently than I, a self-starter, did. It's not that I spent any less or guarded my money but he had a certain way of looking at trends and businesses. My focus in building a company was short-term whereas he seemed more keen in betting on long-term opportunities for he believed they would yield greater results.

The only problem, however, was that he didn't have any start-up capital and his father wouldn't lend a penny.

'My father wants me to work,' he told me. 'According to him, the only way I would understand the value of money is if I learn to earn it.'

At first I didn't believe him but it turned out he was telling me the truth. When his father sent him to Sydney for his master's degree, he told him that he would pay his university fee and for his accommodation. Plus, he would buy him a cellphone and a laptop. He would also get six months of living expenses but beyond that Joshil would have to find some place to work and earn so he could pay for his groceries. In other words, he had to earn his own livelihood.

Another close acquaintance of mine in the MBA course, Girish (name changed), also from India, was the son of an industrialist too. His father, however, had told Girish that he would provide everything and all he had to do was study. The difference between Joshil and Girish was only one: Joshil's family had been rich for the last three generations whereas Girish's father was a self-made man. He didn't want his son to go through the hardships that he had faced.

I have seen it over and over again that often self-made rich parents, or even those upper-middle classes, go the extra mile to ensure that their children have all the comforts in life. Money was very important to them when they were growing up and they ensure that their own children don't need to struggle for it. Whether that's buying the latest model of iPhone or iPad, a Macbook or any other new gadget, their children are provided with the best. The rich, especially those who have been fortunate enough to be well-off for generations, deal with money and their children a little differently. I may be stereotyping here, but when I say self-made, rich parents, I'm not talking about those who go on to become billionaires (they learn the art of parenting somehow, for example Bill Gates, Steve Jobs or Warren Buffet) but those who do reasonably well in their lives.

Coming back to my story, Joshil got a job as a sales person in a retail shop. To cover the weekend rush, the owner hired him at $12/hour, offering him sixteen hours of work. This was enough to pay for his groceries. A year later, after he cleared the first year of his MBA, his father agreed to buy him a car on the condition that he would pay for the fuel himself. Joshil's father would pay for the car and insurance and nothing else.

He called me excitedly. 'We must go out and celebrate,' he said. 'It's my first car ever, that too my own!' We dined outside in a vegetarian restaurant that evening where he told me that the laptop he got the year before was the first one he ever got. He was very happy with his car and he managed to earn a bit more to take care of the fuel, parking expenses and still have money for his groceries.

Another year later, we both completed our MBA. Joshil was hoping to go back to India and run the conglomerate. But his father had different plans.

'I can't let you make mistakes in my company,' he said. 'Go work elsewhere and learn for a few years. I'll then let you work here.' Joshil made a few calls and within the next four weeks, his work visa was arranged with a large French company and he was on a plane to a different city in Australia where he had been hired for a graduate-entry role. For four years, he worked in that company after which his father allowed him to return to India and run their business. Joshil dreamed of running the group and either getting his father's office or a plush new cabin made for him. He was an MBA after all, with four years of management experience in a French multinational company.

Once again, his father had other plans.

'For one year,' he said to Joshil, 'just work under my general manager. You need to know how to report to a boss in the Indian environment and know what challenges your people may face when they'll report to you one day.'

Another year later, his father got him a new car and made him the general manager. Not of the entire company but of a loss-making division in their empire.

'For two years, I'll take care of the staff salaries of this division,' his father said to him. 'I'll also pay other fixed costs such as infrastructure overheads, and I'll give you some operating capital. Turn this division around. If you manage it well, I'll make you a director in the company.'

Joshil was a brilliant guy and now experienced too. He pulled off what his father had asked of him and was later brought onto the company's board. His father knew that giving a role in the company wasn't just about Joshil but about the livelihood of thousands of people associated with their company and the trust of the shareholders. Not to mention a century old brand.

If we are to help our children grow, we must not be afraid of letting them face the challenges of life. We can put the supporting wheels on a cycle when they are learning to ride but there has to come a time when we take one wheel off and then another one, ensuring they learn to balance that bicycle on their own. They will fall, once, twice or a bit more, and in doing so they'll get hurt too, but your job is to be there when they fall, to help them get back up.

Only when we build a sense of self-discipline in their lives will they learn to face and enjoy life boldly. Nick Bilton, a *New York Times* journalist, once asked Steve Jobs what his kids thought about the iPad. After all, the whole world was going crazy about this new gadget and it's only natural to be inquisitive if his family also appreciated it as much as everyone else did.

'Oh, them?' Steve Jobs said, 'They haven't used it yet. iPads are not allowed in the home.'[22]

Numerous studies have shown that depression among youth, notably teenagers, has jumped alarmingly due to an addiction with technology. Executives of some of the largest technology companies in the world have talked about how they greatly limit the use of technology for their children because they have seen the dangers of it first-hand. So, when I say 'Let Them Earn', I don't mean it in a monetary sense. I only mean that just by making someone work for something does not mean we don't love that person. Just because you may not freely cater to all their requirements does not mean you don't care. It simply means that you know better. You know that for a caterpillar to become a butterfly, it must learn to face positive resistance or there will be no growth and it'll continue to remain a grub.

I remember many years ago I was playing chess with my nephew who was upset when he lost the game. He wouldn't say anything directly but I could see his disappointment. I told him that I could take my rook or queen off the board but that wouldn't be a real game. No one in the world would do such a thing and that even if he won under such circumstances, he wouldn't taste the real joy of victory. Instead, I said to him that I could train him, coach him, help him beat me. I could play a game with him where I would share the rationale of my selection of moves and so on. He understood my point and that only made him a better player, not just in chess but in all walks of life.

I am not suggesting that we should make everything hard for them as that would be just as detrimental to their growth. We do have to be sincere, though. Hollow praise do not boost a child's self-esteem. Instead, they confuse a child because they then go out into the world and experience none of what their parents talked about.

A man was late for work in the morning and was rushing to finish his breakfast. Suddenly, the phone rang.

'If it's for me,' he said to his daughter, 'just tell them I'm not home.'

'Okay,' said the daughter.

She picked up the phone and whispered, 'Dad is home right now.'

'Didn't I tell you to say that I was not at home?' the angry father said. 'You want me to lose my job!'

'Relax, Dad. The call was for me.'

PATIENCE
(DELAY GRATIFICATION)

❦

An alternative title to this chapter could have been 'delayed gratification' as it's really about how exercising willpower, enough to wait for a bigger reward in the future by passing up a smaller pleasure can make an enormous difference to how successful a child is going to be in their life. The reason is quite simple: in all walks of life, we need willpower to stick to the choices we make and to resist from harmful ones. I am suggesting that parents can build that culture in their family where by delaying gratification, they help their children build willpower. Better willpower means more control on emotions too. It's incredibly motivational and uplifting for a child when they are able to stick to their resolutions.

'All my resolutions mean nothing,' someone said to me the other day. 'I don't want to smoke or get angry or procrastinate but I end up doing all these things. I want to meditate, exercise and wake up early but no matter what I do, I just don't seem to have the willpower.'

I looked at him quietly because I can't even begin to tell you how common this issue is and how each one of us suffers on account of a lack of willpower.

'It almost feels that I'm born a loser who can't ever stick to his word,' he concluded. 'No one trusts me anymore. Heck, I don't trust myself!'

This happens to most of us on a daily basis. We decide to do one thing but we don't carry it through. We promise ourselves to not feel a certain way or think certain things and yet at the hands of nagging temptations and emotions, we feel overpowered if not completely helpless. Is there a way out? Well, yes. There most certainly is.

In fact, transforming ourselves is not as hard as it may seem at first. It is possible to lead your life and get things done the way you envisage. It is within your reach to shed your past, to walk out of the darkness and into the light. How, you ask?

Away from philosophy, mysticism and spirituality, I have good news for you with practical tips. To begin with, however, I must share with you a famous psychological study first done in 1960. Called the Marshmallow Experiment, it comprised a series of experiments designed by psychologists Walter Mischel and Ebbe B. Ebbesen at Stanford University.

They were studying how a child learns to resist immediate gratification, and they found a creative new way to observe the process in four-year-old children. They would bring the children one at a time into a room, show them a marshmallow, and offer them a deal before leaving them alone in the room. The children could eat the marshmallow whenever they wanted to, but if they held off until the experimenter returned, they would get a second marshmallow to eat along with it. Some children gobbled the marshmallow right away; others tried resisting but couldn't hold out; some managed to wait out the whole fifteen minutes for the bigger reward. The ones who succeeded tended to do so by distracting themselves, which seemed an interesting enough finding at the time of the experiments, in the 1960s.

Much later, though, Mischel discovered something else thanks to a stroke of good fortune. His own daughters happened to attend the same school, on the Stanford University campus, where the marshmallow experiments took place. Long after he finished the experiments and moved on to other topics, Mischel kept hearing from his daughters about their classmates. He noticed that the children who had failed to wait for the extra marshmallow seemed to get in more trouble than the others, both in and out of school. To see if there was a pattern, Mischel and his colleagues tracked down hundreds of veterans of the experiments. They found that the ones who had shown the most willpower at age four went on to get better grades and test scores. The children who had managed to hold out the entire fifteen minutes went on to score 210 points higher on the SAT than the ones who had caved after the first half minute. The children with willpower grew up to become more popular with their peers and their teachers. They earned higher salaries. They had a lower body-mass index, suggesting that they were less prone to gain weight as middle age encroached.

...

People with good self-control seemed exceptionally good at forming and maintaining secure, satisfying attachments to other people. They were shown to be better at empathizing with others and considering things from other people's perspectives. They were more stable emotionally and less prone to anxiety, depression, paranoia, psychoticism, obsessive-compulsive behavior, eating disorders, drinking problems, and other maladies. They got angry less often, and when they did get angry, they were less likely to get aggressive, either verbally or physically.[23]

The Marshmallow Experiment highlights the importance of self-control or delayed gratification. No wonder that Patanjali in his yoga sutras put *yama* (moral restraints) and *niyama* (self-regulation) before anything else. No conscious change is possible without self-control. Here are three simple tips to increase your willpower which will help you tremendously in self-regulation.

Unlike meditation, the Ten Commandments or precepts of hatha-yoga, these are a lot simpler and extremely effective.

Eat Well

Your body uses glucose during self-control. Now you know why many people get cravings for sweets when they are trying to resist a temptation or are fighting a battle with their 'unrestrained' selves. If you are going to eat foods with high glycemic index, such as most starchy and processed foods, packaged snacks, white bread, etc., your body will get a short spurt of energy, but an overall lack of nutrition will make matters worse very soon. Therefore, resist the temptation of a quick top-up and instead focus on eating healthier foods. They include: fresh vegetables, nuts and fresh fruits, cottage cheese and other whole foods. Oh, and don't forget your vitamins! Still better is to supplement your diet with physical exercise. With the right amount of glucose in your blood, you will find it easier to regulate yourself. Try it to believe it.

Set Small Goals

The smaller the goal, the greater the likelihood of attaining it. With each goal you realize, your self-esteem gets a boost which, in turn, leads to stronger willpower. Eating the right foods also fire the right neurotransmitters in the brain which can help one feel positive and self-assured. If you give yourself too big a task without defining smaller, attainable milestones, you are most likely to give up even before you start working towards it seriously. Take one day at a time. Multitasking is the greatest enemy of productivity. My personal view is that doing one thing at a time is more effective and prone to success. Take on something, finish it first and then move to the next one.

Preserve Your Willpower

If the mind is a retailer, then the brain and stomach are distributors of willpower. The body is the only warehouse and consciousness the only supplier. In other words, you only have one original source of willpower to draw from. If you are going to expend your willpower on things that don't matter, you will have little left to use on things that do. When you are trying not to feel guilty, resentful, jealous, angry and so on, when you are trying to resist temptation, you are using willpower. If you focus on self-regulation by eating well, attaining smaller goals and directing your attention to the positives, you won't have to use your energy to win over the negatives. There's no sense in using your willpower to change your feelings (as I wrote in the opening quote). Instead, learn positive distraction to harness your energy.

I read a little something (edited) in Michael Krasny's *Let There Be Laughter*. A young woman went to see Mulla Nasruddin for a peek into her future. She told him that there were two men, Hussein and Aamir, in her life and both loved her deeply. She was unsure whom to marry.

'Please tell me, Mulla,' she asked, 'who will marry me? Who will be the lucky man?'

'Hmm…' Mulla said, stroking his beard, 'Aamir will marry you and Hussein will be the lucky man.'

Mindfulness is the art of being aware of your choices and willpower is the skill of sticking with it, no matter what. You can cultivate and strengthen your willpower as well as help your children do the same. Let them earn their dues and build predictability too so they may lead their blessed lives helping themselves and others.

A young boy approached his father, a manager at a retail shop. The father was engrossed in his newspaper but the boy said he needed to speak about something important.

'Dad,' he said, 'you know Johnny, whose father is a famous surgeon?'

'Yes, what about him?'

'Well, he failed.'

'Too bad!' And he went back to his newspaper. A minute later, the boy pulled the newspaper down a bit, looking at his father.

'And you know Ronny, whose father is a top lawyer? He also failed!'

'That's sad,' the father replied. 'Hey, isn't your result out today too? How did you fare?'

'Even Bob, whose father is a professor and a PhD in physics, failed!'

'Stop telling me about your friends who failed!' the father yelled, putting aside his newspaper. 'Tell me your result! Now!'

'Oh come on! The son of a surgeon failed. The son of a brilliant lawyer failed and that of a bright professor. What are you, an Einstein, that your son will pass?'

EXCELLENCE
(A SENSE OF PERFECTION)

⮜⧔⮞

There's nothing called an extraordinary child, there's just an extraordinary childhood.

A group of aspiring artists once asked the famous Canadian pianist, Glen Gould, the best way to master the piano.

'Give up everything else,' he replied.

This advice was not too far off the mark. When we examine the lives of the greatest achievers in any given field, repeatedly we discover that they devoted their life to the singular pursuit of excellence. That enormous hard work behind the scenes is often deemed as talent, prodigy, genius, fortune and so on. In reality, however, it's tremendous hard work spread out over a long period of time that leads them to mastery. A while back I wrote 'The Secret of Mastery' on my blog, the famous story of Pablo Picasso.

The phenomenal Spanish painter was sitting in a small cafe in France. Waiting for his third cup of coffee, while a smoldering cigarette rested in an ashtray, Picasso was doodling on a paper napkin. Oblivious to him, another patron, a woman from an adjacent table, had been observing keenly. A few minutes later, Picasso put his pencil down, lifted the napkin and stared at it blankly, as if he wasn't pleased or maybe thought it needed more work. He was about to crumple the napkin when the lady spoke.

'Don't!' she hollered, almost startling Picasso. 'I'll take it.'

He gave her a curious look and kept silent a few moments longer than one usually would in a similar situation.

'I'll pay you for it,' the woman continued and reached out for her handbag.

'It's not for gifting or sale,' Picasso said with indifference.

'Oh yeah?' She pulled out her check book. 'Maybe I can offer you a good price!'

'Done. Four million Francs.' This was roughly $10,000.

'That's ridiculous!'

'Well, that's the price.'

'But it only took you a few minutes!'

'No, Madame.' Picasso folded the napkin and put it in his pocket. 'This took me sixty years.'

While growing up, most of us have our sources of inspiration, our role models, people we admire, our super-heroes. These are the people who reached the pinnacle in their respective fields and the world called them geniuses. For they demonstrated not only an extraordinary skill but a great degree of effortlessness too. As if they just sat down and championed their art. Nothing could be further from truth than the assumption that they were born with it or somehow got it all too easy.

Effortlessness in anything comes from immense effort. The more mindful effort we put in any endeavour, the easier it is to become naturally good at it. Whatever you wish to master, be it meditation or basketball or anything at all, be prepared to put in a lot of tiring hours. Keep at it. Mindfully. Keep reviewing and continue working. Gradually, you'll discover that things that seemed difficult, even impossible at first are in fact now well within your reach. If earlier 80 per cent of your time was spent on repetitive and boring aspects of your art, now it is only 20 per cent. The remaining 80 then turns into fun.

What we call genius is often nothing more than dogged determination with years of effort and persistence. Pablo de Sarasate, the famous Spanish violinist and composer, was hailed a genius by critics and followers alike. One day, when someone excitedly brought him a press clipping full of accolades, Sarasate threw the paper aside. 'Huh!' he scoffed. 'For thirty-seven years I've practised fourteen hours a day, and now they call me a genius!'

Even Mozart once wrote to his father, 'People make a great mistake who think that my art has come easily to me. Nobody has devoted so much time and thought to composition as I.'

And this is not just about Mozart or Picasso but anyone who has ever conquered the heights of greatness has done so with ruthless self-discipline and hard work. While spiritual texts talk about leading a balanced life, one of moderation, the truth is that those who are in a state of flow, walking the path with a single-minded focus, are anything but balanced in how they spend their time. When they are not working on what they are passionate about, they are thinking about it.

The foundation of the competence and confidence of geniuses is built on a monumental and consistent effort spread out over a prolonged period of time. What is even more remarkable is that many of them overcame extraordinary obstacles in their path. Which, if I may say, is perfectly understandable because the bigger your goal, the greater the hurdles. A rocket needs a massive thrust during its launch but once it's in space, it not just derives energy from its own fuel but also from the gravity of other planets. The same is the case with masters. Those who are persistent reach cruise mode eventually, a state where everything around them works in harmony and helps them in attaining an exalted state of super-consciousness. By super-consciousness, I don't mean anything mystical but simply a state where you discover your inner potential, a higher state of intuitive understanding. It is from such a place that creativity flows unimpeded like the Ganges from the Himalayas.

A complex imported machine broke down in a semiconductor factory, bringing the entire production to a halt. The mere sight of the machine with thousands of nuts and bolts, cogs and gears, wires and all was daunting enough to scare their best engineers. The company was losing money by the second and no one in the group could find a solution. Finally, an expert was flown in. He examined the machine, replaced a small screw and fixed the problem in five minutes. A week later, the company execs were fuming after receiving a bill of $10,000.

They wrote back to him demanding a breakdown of the exorbitant fee for a job that took practically no time. The engineer sent a new invoice with the following line items:

Cost of screw: $2.00
Replacing the screw: $20.00
Knowing which screw to replace: $9,978.

All of us have some level of access to similar mental and physical resources to build our lives but it's how we put them to use that determines whether we are standing on the stage or sitting in the audience – though both may be enjoying themselves equally. The wisdom to value every moment of our lives and the discipline to spend it judiciously are at the core of becoming a genius.

Mastery of any art, craft or skill is not the prerogative of a fortunate few but the birthright of every single individual. There's no fun in being mediocre. Between mastery and mediocrity, we spend an equal amount of time anyway with just a small difference. A master spends all his/her time on the one thing that matters whereas a mediocre person devotes his to things that don't. Both have only twenty-four hours in a day.

As a parent, the question is how do you inspire your child to devote wholeheartedly to mastering a skill? How do you inform them that it will do them much good? While it may or may not result in the attainment of their material goals, it will lead to a more fulfilling life. While it's true that many talented people in human history led a depressed and a lonely life, it is also true that an overwhelming majority of great people lived a life of glory, and more importantly, they lived in what Mihaly Csikszentmihalyi, famous researcher and psychologist, called 'a state of flow'.[24]

The idea behind sharing this story and others is not that we turn our children into people hungry for money, power and fame, but that we help them see their spiritual side, the world's spiritual side. This in turn will help them be better human beings, thus raising the overall happiness quotient of our world. Here, it is quite important for me to spell out clearly beforehand: by spiritual, I don't mean religious. By spiritual, I don't mean to say that pursuing material goals in life is not a spiritual act. Instead, I simply mean that when we do any act with full awareness, wholeheartedly and with sincerity, when our intention behind that action is not merely for personal welfare but of others too, we are performing a spiritual act.

Spirituality is not something we can cram into a child's mind, nor is it something we can teach using books or essays, but something they learn on their own. And that learning only happens in an environment that's conducive to spiritual growth. A functional family can provide that environment. If your children are not afraid to share their feelings with you, if you allow them to make some mistakes, if they are encouraged to speak the truth, if you have moments of laughter with them, if there's a feeling of togetherness, you can be certain that your children are going to lead a spiritual life.

The question that now arises is of how to create that environment in a family where individuality is fostered, where family members look forward to dining together and supporting each other. It begins with good parenting.

And good parenting is not just about the parents' relationship with their children but also with each other and other people in the world. No matter what your past or how your own childhood was, you *can* have a family where there are more moments of joy than stress.

NURTURE

MINDFULNESS
(WHAT ARE YOU UP TO?)

The secret of great parenting is quite simple: mindfulness. And it begins by being aware of your speech. If you are mindful of what you speak, how much you speak, when you speak, and the tone you use, 90 per cent of the job is done. The other 10 per cent no one knows – remember the pastor's commandments in the first chapter?

If you want anything done from anyone without getting into a conflict, make it look like it's their idea. The moment you accomplish this feat, the other person will willingly and gladly do what you want. This is also the secret to great leadership. Not by showering hollow praises or flattering someone – though inordinate highlighting of their virtues may be required to motivate them at times – but by championing the art of speech which is basically knowing what, when, where, how and how much to say.

The greatest damage you do in a relationship is not necessarily with your actions but with your words. Most people wreck their relationships by saying the wrong thing at the wrong time. I meet parents who are doing everything for their children, providing them with the best education, expensive gadgets, new cars, generous pocket money and so on and yet their kids seem to remain defiant.

Once Buddha got upset with a man called Devadutta. In front of the whole congregation, Buddha pulled him aside and dismissed him by saying, 'Devadutta, you will burn in hell.' Many people who were present there were shocked, to say the least. They had never heard or seen Buddha speak like this to anyone. Those who opposed Buddha got the perfect opportunity to prove that he didn't practise his own teachings. They waited for the right time and the right person to confront Buddha.

Finally, they convinced a prince called Abhaya to ask Buddha if he ever spoke harsh and bitter words. If Buddha was to say he hadn't, this would prove him a liar because clearly he had, and if he replied saying he did speak harshly, this would make him an ordinary man, like everyone else who uses harsh words when angry.

'Do you ever speak harsh and bitter words?' Devadutta asked Buddha in a congregation of 500 monks and observers.

Buddha went quiet for a few minutes before saying, 'There's no categorical "yes" or "no" answer to your question.'

'But, Devadutta,' Buddha added, 'I will tell you how Tathagata chooses his words.'

Buddha almost always referred to himself in the third person as Tathagata, the one who has gone beyond. In his discourse, Buddha explained six considerations of speech; call them six tests if you will. If you were to make this teaching your life's core operating philosophy, not just in parenting but in all spheres and kinds of relationship, you will never find yourself hurting the other person. So, Buddha said:

> *In the case of words, Prince, that the Tathagata knows to be un-factual, untrue, unbeneficial (or: not connected with the goal), unendearing and disagreeable to others, he does not say them.*

If the words are not factual, true, beneficial, endearing or agreeable, there's no sense in using such words. It's a no-brainer. And yet, all the time, especially in conflict, there comes a point that both parties go off tangent. It's no longer about getting your point across. Instead, the focus shifts to 'making a point' and a sort of race starts about who can hurt the other person more with their words. For example, I once heard a father scold his young son in a restaurant who spilled his drink on the table.

'Why can't you ever eat without making a mess?' he was telling his son, trying hard to not raise his voice. 'Even a dog eats better than you. It's a nightmare to ever take you out.'

The words *why can't you ever eat without making a mess*, can't possibly be true or factual. There must be a time when this child hadn't made a mess. With words like this, you are not communicating but attacking. Further, comparing him to a dog is not only unendearing and disagreeable, but downright insulting and demeaning. When we speak words that fail the first test (of words being factual, true, beneficial, endearing and agreeable), we can't possibly hope for the child to trust us or enjoy our company.

Buddha continued:

> In the case of words that the Tathagata knows to be factual, true, unbeneficial, unendearing and disagreeable to others, he does not say them.

Even if the words are true and factual, it does not mean we have to say them. Particularly if such words are not endearing and agreeable (which, often enough, even true and factual words are not). But most importantly, the question to be asked is whether those words are beneficial. If it's not going to benefit the listener in any way, what is the sense in using such speech? After all, when you reprimand a child, it's not just for the sake of it, right? The idea is to ensure that such behaviour from a child is not repeated because somewhere, as a parent, you believe that it is not good for them. And if that's the intention, speaking unbeneficial words is not going to fulfil it.

All the time I hear parents saying to their children things like 'you are short', 'you are fat', 'you are lazy', 'you are ungrateful' and so on. Do you really believe that they benefit the child at all? I am not suggesting that we can't speak the truth, on the contrary, we should only speak sincere words as much as possible but that does not mean that all true and factual statements are beneficial too. I read somewhere that some people are so brutally honest, it almost seems they enjoy more being brutal than truthful. But what if the words are actually beneficial to them? Well, let's see what Buddha said in his next statement to the prince.

> In the case of words that the Tathagata knows to be factual, true, beneficial, but un-endearing and disagreeable to others, he has a sense of the proper time for saying them.

Now the words are true, beneficial, factual but they are not endearing or agreeable. Far from it. They are now confrontational. You are a parent and it's your job to tell the truth. How will the child improve if you are only going to say words that are endearing and agreeable? A lot of the time what's beneficial for them is not necessarily what they want to hear. Fair enough. Buddha said that when such is the case, one must have a proper sense and time for saying them. That is, wait for the right moment.

Imagine you are invited to your friend's daughter's birthday party. She's a bright girl who is an extremely good tennis player and scores straight A's in school. You go there with your spouse and your son who's a distracted teenager who could do with some more focus and hard work in life. You know it *and* your son knows it. In fact, everyone in the family knows it. The mood is very party-like at the gathering and everyone seems to be having fun. Just then, a few words are spoken about the birthday girl, about her achievements and so on.

You turn to your son and say, 'Why can't you be like her? You never take anything seriously. All your friends seem to be doing better than you. When will you start studying with more focus?'

What you are saying may be true, factual and beneficial but the words are unendearing and disagreeable, though the choice of words in the dialogue above is not the best. A better way to communicate would be: *Are you enjoying the party? She's a nice girl, very studious and hardworking …* and leave it at that. In other words, highlight a positive trait of someone and let your child absorb it. Less is more. This is anyway not the time or the place to speak such a thing. Besides, any tone you choose in a gathering like this to reprimand your child is likely to be the wrong tone. What is the objective of telling your child to be like her in this instance? Whatever it may, however noble, it will not go through to them. There is always a way of saying what you want to say and all it takes is a bit of sensitivity and mindfulness. How would I like to hear it if I was in the other person's shoes? You will be surprised how posing this simple question to yourself before you speak will alter your selection of words and the manner in which you deliver them. What about the reverse, you ask? That is, what if you just want to say something to boost their spirits? Those words which may or may not be true. What would Buddha do in your place? Here are the next two filters:

> In the case of words that the Tathagata knows to be un-factual, untrue, unbeneficial, but endearing and agreeable to others, he does not say them.
>
> In the case of words that the Tathagata knows to be factual, true, unbeneficial, but endearing and agreeable to others, he does not say them.

Buddha's criteria is quite clear; no matter how factual, true (or otherwise), endearing and agreeable the words maybe, if they are not beneficial, they are not going to help your child. And even when the words are beneficial, we still have to take into consideration our timing and manner of saying such words. Let's say you are a coach and training an archer to compete in the Olympics. You've worked very hard with your pupil and you know she has immense potential. She's about to take aim when you shout, 'I know you can do it! You are my best pupil, the greatest archer I've ever known.'

Your words may be true and factual and the student is certainly finding them endearing and agreeable, but the timing of speaking such words only makes them unbeneficial. She's not going to benefit from these words under the given circumstances.

I remember a girl came to me last year and said, 'My parents are very good but that's the whole problem. They are always praising me.'

I looked at her intriguingly because I wasn't quite sure where this was going or what she meant.

'But I know,' she added, 'they are saying all that to just make me feel good. That creates so much pressure in my mind.'

'Give me an example,' I said.

'Just the other day, they sat me down after I failed in one of my subjects and kept telling me that how they were so proud of me and that they were sure I could top if I wanted. How come they are proud of me? What have I done? And, of course, I want to top but I can barely pass. They create so much pressure by telling me all these things that just aren't true and it puts a tremendous burden on me to meet their expectations.'

In the previous chapter, I talked about authenticity and I guess that's what I mean. If your words are not sincere, they'll lose their value and ring hollow to the child.

There's a famous story that Mahatma Gandhi narrated once. A woman took her son to Gandhi and complained that he ate excessive raw sugar. She'd tried everything but nothing made him stop. She told Gandhi she had come to him with great hope and asked for his blessings.

'Come after six months,' Gandhi said. 'I'll rid your child of the habit of eating sugar.'

She counted her days with great eagerness and went to Gandhi exactly six months later.

'Come here, my son,' Gandhi said, and lovingly pulled the boy to him. 'Don't eat sugar, alright? It's not good for you.'

The boy nodded.

'So, do you promise me?' Gandhi asked him.

He gave Gandhi his word that he would refrain from eating raw sugar. The mother, however, remained unconvinced and looked at Gandhi askance.

'Why on earth,' she said to Gandhi, 'would you make me wait six months if you just had to give this simple instruction?'

'Well,' Gandhi replied, 'until six months ago, I used to consume a lot of sugar myself. So, first I quit and then gave the same advice to this boy. Now my words will have an impact on him.'

If your words are sincere then alone will they benefit your child. Here's my definition of sincere words:

authentic words spoken at the right time in a soft tone. However, what if the words you wish to speak are true, factual, beneficial, endearing and agreeable? They meet all the conditions; would you say such words? Here's Buddha's take:

> *In the case of words that the Tathagata knows to be factual, true, beneficial, and endearing and agreeable to others, he has a sense of the proper time for saying them. Why is that? Because the Tathagata has compassion for living beings.*[25]

That sums it up pretty nicely: no matter what you wish to say, choose an appropriate time and say it politely. Somebody comes home really tired in the evening, let that person rest a bit, or wait till the next day; let them take a breather before you give them the bad news. Everybody comes home to relax. If there is no peace at home, where will one go? I think the home is one such environment where keeping it joyous and peaceful as a matter of commitment helps a child more than anything else.

It all may sound a bit philosophical but the truth is it's entirely doable. It's a matter of building a family culture, building daily habits. I remember when we were growing up, my parents would return home together from work every evening. As a matter of rule, one out of the three of us children was required to ask them if they wanted fresh lime water and if there was no lime that day, then at least bring them a glass of water each. We were not allowed to bombard them with the events of our day or questions for thirty minutes. And the good thing is that they would not bug us with any questions whenever we came home after a long day either.

Nothing sets a better example than action. Do it repeatedly and your children will start following you sooner or later. Do it gently and joyously and they'll certainly follow suit far sooner than you can imagine.

Open, polite and honest communication are certain attributes I've observed that make great families great.

"*Dear, I hope you don't think I'm too old-fashioned, but do you think you could call me 'Grandmother' or 'Grandma' instead of 'Butt-Head'?*"

CORE VALUES
(RULES OF ENGAGEMENT)

~~ꞙꝍꞙ~~

'I've always been a good parent and supported my children at every step,' a somewhat distressed parent said to me a few weeks ago, 'and yet, they don't really respect me. They are struggling in their lives and tell me that I've been a terrible father. I don't get it; I always loved them, allowed them to do whatever they wanted. They got the best clothes, gadgets and so on. I don't think I cheated anyone, I've been God-fearing. I never thought my kids would end up like this. Where did I go wrong?'

I've been asked similar questions a number of times. What's truly remarkable is that most kids and parents only mean well. They try too hard. Kids want their parents to be proud of them and vice-versa. So, where is the mismatch? I hear it all the time that such-and-such person is a bad father or mother, that they are irreligious, immoral, etc., and yet their families are flourishing and their kids are doing great. Where's the justice in that?

In my view, this is the wrong way to look at life. Admittedly, I'm no authority when it comes to parenting. I'm a monk, remember? But having personally met a few thousand parents and children in the last few years, however, I'm happy to share some thoughts based on my observations and diagnosis of life. Let me begin with a story from Stephen Hodge's *Zen Master Class*.

Several of the monks at Dogen's monastery had noticed a deer grazing nearby. They began to feed it scraps of food. After some time the deer started trusting them and would eat out of their hands. Having taken to heart Dogen's teachings about compassion, the monks were pleased with themselves. However, Dogen himself was less happy when he heard about the deer. When a suitable opportunity arose, he threw sticks and stones at the deer, which ran away frightened.

The monks were scandalized by Dogen's actions and confronted him, demanding an explanation. 'We were kindly feeding the deer, but you have cruelly thrown stones at it so it no longer visits.'

'So, you think you were being compassionate, do you?' Dogen replied. 'It is dangerous for a deer to become accustomed to people.'

The monks protested, 'We would never do anything to hurt it. We were just feeding it.'

'No, you didn't intend to hurt the deer, but what if the next person your tame deer met was a hunter?'

The same goes for a parent–child bond as well. Giving them whatever they ask for does not necessarily make one a good parent. Kids have a lot of demands. Everyone does. But that doesn't mean that everything they desire is right for them. I'm not suggesting, even for a moment, that you become a harsh parent. It is, however, important to know where and when to be firm. If you keep children in touch with reality, it'll be much easier for them to adjust to the real world when they step out.

Being God-fearing, moral, genuine means you are a good person. If you are successful at work, you are a competent worker. If you love and care for your partner, it shows you are a good husband or wife. Your competency in any area will bring you corresponding rewards. But none of this implies that you are a good parent. There is no doubt that these factors contribute to the well-being of a family. When it comes to sound parenting, however, there's certainly more to it than providing your children with whatever they want.

As in the anecdote above, a good parent must know when and where to be firm. To love is to not do whatever they want you to. That has never made anyone happy in the long term anyway. Instead, to love is to stand your ground where needed – only for the betterment of your children. They will express their displeasure and it requires a strong heart to see a child sad, but they'll thank you later. Once again, I say, you don't have to be harsh. There's no need to shout, argue violently, or be mad at them. You can be gentle and still be firm.

Be compassionate, be firm, but do so mindfully. Just remember that no one wants to fail, no one wants to be angry or sad. Kids have just as much pressure and stress in their lives as their parents. So go a little easy, but again do so mindfully. While growing up, I don't have even any recollection of my mother ever shouting or getting angry and yet, there were many instances when she was firm. One rule was that our report cards, which required a parent's signature, would be signed by our father, for example. At times, like when the score in maths or physics was the same as my dog's age, we whined and complained but mother wouldn't relent. It was non-negotiable. Father would always need to be the one to sign. Eventually, we understood and trained ourselves to score better.

'I got my report card, Dad,' fourteen-year-old Johnny said. He had scored rather poorly and feared a severe reprimand. His father grabbed his specs to read the report card.

'And look what else I found, Dad!' Johnny handed him a soiled paper. 'In the attic, I also chanced upon your report card when you were fourteen. We have scored at par!' 'Hmm...' his father said, comparing his own report card with his son's. 'You are absolutely right, Johnny. They almost look identical.'

Johnny beamed triumphantly.

'Therefore, son,' his father said, reaching out to his slipper, 'it's only reasonable that I give you what my father gave me.'

No, Johnny didn't get an iPhone or an Xbox. And no, this is not an example of parental compassion. Humour aside, the truth is that an unexpected punishment damages the relationship because the quantum of such penalty is always debatable. The terms of non-performance must be negotiated beforehand, so both kids and parents know exactly what is expected from each other. It sounds obvious but you'll be surprised to see how many parents start lecturing instead of simply and gently stating their expectations. I call it OLD – Obsessive Lecture Disorder. It has never helped anyone. From what I have gathered, the older a parent, more serious the OLD. A while ago I wrote that pain is inevitable but suffering is optional. In the same vein, growing old is inevitable but OLD is optional. Be gentle.

If you tackle OLD with mindfulness, understanding and practising parental compassion, the quality of your relationship will improve immensely. They will grow up to be more fulfilled adults, more together, making our world a better place. Mindful compassion or soft discipline is not enough on its own, though. No one said it would be easy. There are five more aspects of good parenting:

Compassion (*Karuna*)

The first one: compassion (*karuna*) — I will talk of the remaining ones but will begin with the most important one. As has become our wont, sort of, let me share a quick story first.

A contract worker had to do a double shift at work. He came home knackered and irritated (you all know that feeling).

'Dad,' his six-year-old son said, 'how much do you make an hour?'

'Not now, son,' he said. 'Besides, you should know that it's a rude question.'

'But I just wanna know!

'What the hell!' the man hollered. 'Your tired father comes home and rather than giving me a hug, you ask me a dumb question like this.'

'But I want to buy something urgently,' the boy persisted.

'You selfish little weed!' The father lost it completely. 'Get lost!'

'But—'

'No arguments! Get back to your room.'

The boy stood there with his head hung low. His eyes welled up and a tear trickled down.

'Go to your room, I said! Now!'

The son quietly walked back to his room and shut the door behind him.

At night, after the father had had his dinner and calmed down, he went to the little boy.

'I'm sorry, son,' he said. 'I was very tired and I don't know what came over me. What do you want to buy?'

'First tell me how much you make,' the boy said again, timidly. '$20 an hour.'

Reaching under his pillow, he pulled out some money. Crumpled $1 bills, some nickels and dimes that he had been saving for weeks.

'Here's $10, Dad,' he said, putting the money in his hands. 'Will you play with me for thirty minutes?'

The father's enraged reaction to the first question might seem unreasonable but that's exactly what anger is: unreasonable. In hindsight, after you've calmed down, you see how it was excessive or unjust but while experiencing the emotion, it feels right. I haven't cited this story to highlight anger but for an entirely different reason, which now leads me to the second principle of parenting.

Time (*Samaya*)

The most important question is, do you have time for parenting? Luxuries, the best education, gadgets, these do not make up for time. Good parenting requires that you give your children time. I know it's demanding at work and you come home tired and have no energy to even utter a word, but to make a 'good parent' you have to give 'good time'.

This may mean cutting down on your TV time or other activities and spending more time with your child. Or it could be that you curtail your professional ambitions and place your family higher on the priority list. A family doesn't need to be in a million-dollar home to be happy. You don't have to take out a big mortgage or have a premium car. Millions of people communicate comfortably without an iPhone. You get the idea.

It's not just true for parenting but everything. Whatever you want to nurture, you have to devote time to it. Giving time to angry thoughts only grows that anger further. Give your time to loving thoughts and watch the love grow. If you want to learn anything, give it time.

Friendship (*Maitri*)

Ordinarily, *maitri* is referred to as loving-kindness. Its literal meaning is friendship. Anything coming from or given by a friend or even belonging to a friend is *maitri*. With friends, we can pour our hearts out without being judged. If your children can come home and share their pains and sorrows without the fear of reprisal or penalties, the tree of friendship will take deep roots.

And this is true not just for a parent and child but all relationships. Friendship is the fuel. The lack of *maitri*, where two people are more focused on keeping things from each other than sharing them, gives rise to permanent undercurrents of tension and discomfort. As I have written many a time earlier, being a friend doesn't mean you always say 'yes'. On the contrary, it means to be able to say 'no' in a positive way. It is to disagree while maintaining a healthy relationship. It is not as hard as it may sound in a sincere relationship.

Joy (*Mudita*)

Mudita is a simple word with a straightforward meaning: joy. Even if you have compassion and are devoting time to parenting *and* there's a degree of friendship but your relationship lacks joy, it'll get very difficult very quickly. The joy of celebrating victories, of having a family, of laughing away at the pranks of life. The heart to live through failures. The courage to forgive and seek forgiveness. A sort of openness and honesty allows you to be comfortable with those around you.

If most conversations with your kids revolve around lecturing them, however soft or positive you think you may sound, even as friends, the joy in your relationship will evaporate in no time. They'll start avoiding you. Most parents have this strong tendency to keep showering advice on their children. Of course, it's done with the right intention but would you feel joyous having a 'friendly' boss who keeps telling you how to become better? Sometimes, no advice is the best advice.

Here's the secret of joy in a relationship: don't take yourself too seriously.

Freedom (*Upeksha*)

Many scholars like Thich Nhat Hanh define *upeksha* as equanimity or freedom. Perhaps, the true test of trust in a relationship is how much freedom it grants, and also how such privilege is used. There's another meaning of *upeksha*, though: patience. And patience is something that most parents possess and lose in abundance — strangely enough, sometimes at the same time.

'Do you know when Abraham Lincoln was of your age he studied under the street lamps?' This was what a father said to his fourteen-year-old every time he scolded him, which was nearly everyday. He thought it would inspire his child. For months, the boy listened to the same argument over and over again.

One day he couldn't take it anymore and shot back. 'Dad,' he said, 'do you know when Abraham Lincoln was of your age, he was the president of the United States of America?'

Be patient. Understand that when you were fifteen or twenty, you were going through similar challenges they are facing now. You also loved lazing around, waking up late perhaps, eating junk food and so on. Maybe there were times when you told lies, bunked classes and fooled around. This is all part of growing up.

As parents, you only mean well but you can't teach them everything. And you shouldn't try to. For there are certain lessons only life can impart. And life never transmits a lesson alone. It does so *with* time. We can do the best we can and the rest must be left to time. The flower of life unfolds eventually. Rushing it is wrecking it.

Be patient. Be gentle. Be kind. Take it easy.

*"Now, we can get all those repressed memories
the easy way or the hard way."*

PREDICTABILITY
(YOU KNOW WHAT...)

꧁◈꧂

How many times have you felt that motivating a child with a certain reward (their favourite video game, toy, gadget) or threatening them with punishment fails to evoke the right sentiment in them or triggers the expected behaviour? Perhaps all the time, right? It nearly never works to entice a child to do a certain thing by offering them a financial or a material reward. If it did, all salespeople in every company would be ogling over the incentives that come with higher sales.

Don't get me wrong, it's possible to offer a child $10 and get him or her to do the dishes or mow the lawn. What is a bit more far-fetched is to offer them a reward of $500 and ask them to do that job for fifty weeks in a row and then expect them to do it. The basis of human motivation and participation, without fail, is a reward. Often though, it's not financial or material – think about how active people are on social media without any material gain in return.

Before I go further into the theory of motivation or extracting a desired behaviour from a child, I would like to share an interesting case study I came across in Dan Ariely's *The Upside of Irrationality*. Dan's own story of grit and survival following a freak accident is quite inspirational too, offering great insight into human resilience and adaptability:

> *More than a century ago, psychologists Robert Yerkes and John Dodson performed different versions of this basic experiment in an effort to find out two things about rats: how fast they could learn and, more important, what intensity of electric shocks would motivate them to learn fastest. We could easily assume that as the intensity of the shocks increased, so would the rats' motivation to learn. When the shocks were very mild, the rats would simply mosey along, unmotivated by the occasional painless jolt. But as the intensity of the shocks and discomfort increased, the scientists thought the rats would feel as though they were under enemy fire and would therefore be more motivated to learn more quickly. Following this logic we would assume that when the rats really wanted to avoid the most intense shocks, they would learn the fastest.*
>
> *We are usually quick to assume that there is a link between the magnitude of the incentive and the ability to perform better. It seems reasonable that the more motivated we are to achieve something, the harder we will work to reach our goal, and that this increased effort will ultimately move us closer to our objective. This, after all, is part of the rationale behind paying*

stockbrokers and CEOs sky-high bonuses: offer people a very large bonus, and they will be motivated to work and perform at very high levels.

Sometimes our intuitions about the links between motivation and performance (and, more generally, our behaviour) are accurate; at other times, reality and intuition just don't jibe. In Yerkes and Dodson's case, some of the results aligned with what most of us might expect, while others did not. When the shocks were very weak, the rats were not very motivated, and, as a consequence, they learnt slowly. When the shocks were of medium intensity, the rats were more motivated to quickly figure out the rules of the cage, and they learnt faster. Up to this point, the results fit with our intuitions about the relationship between motivation and performance.

But here was the catch: when the shock intensity was very high, the rats performed worse! Admittedly, it is difficult to get inside a rat's mind, but it seemed that when the intensity of the shocks was at its highest, the rats could not focus on anything other than their fear of the shock. Paralyzed by terror, they had trouble remembering which parts of the cage were safe and which were not and, so, were unable to figure out how their environment was structured.[26]

'My parents are telling me that they would buy me a car if I cleared the engineering entrance examination,' a boy said to me almost seven years ago. 'But this offer hasn't lured me. I'm already trying and I know I can't clear it. It's not for me.'

'Why do you think you can't clear it?' I asked.

'Because I don't want to do it!'

'Oh!' I was surprised because his parents – whom I'd met a few times earlier – had seemed quite certain that not only would their son would clear the entrance examination, but that it was a given that he would get a high rank. After all, they'd told me, he loved cars and always took out his father's car and the lure of his own car would certainly motivate him. 'So, what do you want to do if not engineering?'

'I want to play the guitar.'

'Right! And you intend to make a living out of playing the guitar?'

He just shrugged and when I persisted that I just wanted to know out of curiosity, he countered saying I thought it wasn't possible to be a professional guitarist.

'Of course, it's possible! I'm not discouraging you from pursuing the guitar. I just want to know if that's what you want to do.'

'Yes.'

'How many hours do you practice in a week?'

'There's no set routine, I just play whenever I feel like.'

'Roughly, the number of hours?'

'Two to three.'

'In a day or a week?'

'Week.'

I told him that if he was this casual about his passion, perhaps it wasn't passion but fleeting infatuation.

'With just two to three hours a week,' I said to him, 'won't make you a pro.'

He shrugged again and said, 'That's okay.'

'And how do you plan to make a living then?'

'It won't be a problem,' he spoke with the usual conviction of a teenager, 'I'll just join my father's business.'

I chuckled. 'Then you and I both know that we are wasting our time here because deep inside, you've already made up your mind to work in his business.' 'Maybe.' And he laughed.

I saw nothing wrong with this boy, just that he was distant from reality, and when a child exhibits such ignorance about real life, I'm sorry to tell you but it shows a clear lack of good parenting. For good parenting does not mean that you provide utmost comforts to your child or you keep them insulated from the real world, it means exposing your child to the truth, little by little. There are many ways in which you can make a child aware of what they need to know. The more they are in touch with the truth, the more grounded they will be.

When a child is not motivated or is lazy, any lure of rewards is not going to build motivation. To encourage them to walk a certain path in life, they have to be trained from a young age. One such way is that parents talk about some of the challenges they are facing in their lives in front of their children. It should not be done in a way that seems you're complaining but more like talking amongst yourselves. Children overhear more than they hear. They learn more by this than by direct lectures at home.

I am not saying that ours was the perfect household when we were growing up. We faced the challenges of any other middle-class family, but one thing that helped us tremendously was that we knew what to expect. I don't ever remember my father luring me with a reward in order to do something. When I asked him for a portable keyboard or my first video game, he didn't say 'do this' or 'do that' and then I'll buy for you. Instead, he bought it and showed faith in me. Plus, I knew he was strict enough to take all that away if I just sat around and wasted my time. He had funded his own education with great difficulty and hard-labour and his life's dream was to make sure that his three children received a good education. But he realized not everyone was keen to become an engineer or a doctor and he was okay with it, provided we didn't sit around and do nothing (although now that's exactly what I teach people in meditation: to sit and do nothing … just kidding). He said it was okay to relax but wasting time was not an option. Either master some skill or an art or get traditional education or if we weren't keen to invest in our time in any of these, he told us to take up a job. Sitting at home and watching TV all day would not be allowed. He told us he didn't have the funds to support us forever.

So, our motivation was to have a better life and he had made amply clear that if we wanted one, we had to build it and work for it. This sense of reality didn't come overnight. It was based on how we saw him working hard not just at work but for his family. He would cook hot breakfast for my mother and always tell her that since she was going to make it for everyone else, it was important that she had her breakfast first. He would join her in the kitchen every single evening and help her out saying she was also a working lady, and that it was his job as the husband to be there for her. At dinner, he would make hot chapatis for her. When we were young, he told my mother to visit all the religious places she wanted to. He would say, 'When you are old, you may not have the desire or the energy and when the children are in their teens, you may not have the time. Now that they are young and small, I can take care of them and you can take some time off. This will give you a break.' If this is how he lived his life, we well knew what was expected of us. And it made things very easy when you know clearly what is expected from you.

Predictability. That's the key.

When parents act in an unpredictable fashion, it not only adversely impacts a child's development but also creates a gap between the parent and the child. And by predictability, I don't mean that parents can't be spontaneous. I simply mean that children should know what to expect and somewhere they need to be okay with it or at least have accepted it. This is possible if they are involved in the stage when rules are set and they are absolutely clear about what they can and can't do and the consequences of these actions thereof. For example, your child yells at you and you take away his video game. 'You can't play it for two days,' you say to him. 'And if it happens the next time, it will be for a week!'

From your perspective, you might think that you gave a light punishment and made clear the repercussions of repeating a certain behaviour. But the truth is that it's not necessarily what your child feels. He may think that taking away his video game for two hours would have been enough, for example. But had you negotiated in advance when things were calm at home or when you bought him the game, he would be more accepting and the punishment would have made greater sense to him. If you are going to announce a punishment, even future punishment, when things are tense, when you are confronting, it's not going to work. There's going to be a revolt. If they are allowed to speak up, they will or they will do it silently. This deteriorates a relationship.

Sit down and negotiate rules and keep some room for laxity. Take it easy. Be firm but be gentle. The reverse of a punishment is equally important, that is praise. If you praise your child saying, 'I'm very proud of you, you are so intelligent' or 'you are so talented', and so on, it is yet another poor strategy. This does not tell the child anything nor does she know what to do to earn more praise. If you want to appreciate, then appreciate the action along with an attribute and not the outcome. If you cite a specific instance, that's even better. For example, let's say your child scores second place in her school. Rather than saying 'I am so proud of you for coming second, it's okay if you didn't come first, you can try harder next time', it's more effective to say 'I'm so proud of you that you worked with such discipline, putting in three hours every day. I was so impressed when you skipped going to the excursion and chose to study.' That, coming first or second matters but not in the grand scheme of things, hard work with self-discipline is more important and that they did so well.

In other words, an outcome is not always in our hands and praising the outcome puts great burden on the child to compete where not necessary and to always weigh his or her success in relation to their standing against others. Whatever you praise, you are going to encourage that behaviour. Keep the praise reasonable and real if you wish to keep it effective.

In the story of the boy I cited earlier in this chapter, he told me that his parents said they were so proud of him and that he played the guitar very well. When I prodded further, it turned out he was barely a beginner. His dream and aspiration was there. He was already eighteen and had not made any serious effort to learn or play the instrument and yet, his parents' excessive praise created a sense of insecurity in him. He knew he didn't play that well. He thought he could just join his father's business whereas his father had been telling me how he had been trying to exit his debt-ridden business. The son had no clue about this. In case you are wondering, he did not pass the entrance examination. Seven years later, nearly twenty-six, he is still learning guitar two or three hours a week. He has his own car. It took him five years to complete a three-year degree in humanities. His parents find it impossible to speak to him. In their words, 'He treats us like shit, he speaks to us like he hates us.' Nearly all their assets are mortgaged because the business has even more debt now than it did earlier. The parents asked me if someone had performed some black magic on them.

'It's not a case of black magic,' I said to the parents, 'the magic of good parenting is missing.'

They told me that so many times they tried to get him involved in their business but he's just not interested. 'I don't like your way of doing business or your business itself,' he told them. 'I'll start my own one day and build a world-class company.'

The parents were at their wits' end and quite understandably because this was long coming. Situations like these don't come up overnight. A delicate balance between being a friend and being a parent is a must if a child has to make any real progress in life. I am not saying that just be harsh or just be soft, at least be predictable and be real. This will help the child know the ground reality of your home and the world. It will teach them to lead responsible lives and that if they are to realize their dreams, a lot will depend on their own effort.

To help a child lead a more responsible life is a parent's job. To make them aware of the reality when they are growing up is also a parent's job. You will be amazed at what all they can do if you nurture them and not just protect them. Plants that belong indoors wither away in external conditions. This is a wild world, if you are unctuous in your praise or unpredictable in your rage, you are not helping your child.

When I was in Grade 7 in school, I was asked to deliver a speech on behalf of nearly 2000 students on the eve of Children's Day which my teacher had helped me write at the time. The speech ended with a beautiful passage:

'Help us in taking small steps so we may make giant leaps. Allow us to make some minor decisions so we may learn to take major ones. Let us make small mistakes so we may learn to avoid bigger ones.'

Son: For $20, I'll be good.
Father: Oh, yeah? When I was your age, I was good for nothing.

DIALOGUE
(HELP, NOT MAKE, THEM UNDERSTAND)

~✦~

One day I was walking from my cottage to the meeting room in my ashram where I was to meet roughly sixty people over the next three hours. Just outside my meeting room, a group of young children stopped me. They were all between the ages of fourteen and nineteen.

'Swamiji,' one of them said, 'we need to talk to you.'

'Is everything okay?' I asked out of concern. For a moment, I thought maybe there was an emergency of some kind or they needed to apprise me of something that they couldn't speak to me in public about.

'Yes,' one of the girls said, 'but we must speak to you.'

'But I already met each one of you yesterday!' I pointed to the long queue of people I was to meet as per my schedule.

'We know,' they insisted, 'but this is quite important.' I asked them if they could write a letter instead or speak to my PA to schedule something later but they were insistent that they needed to see me that very day. Naturally, I relented and asked them to see me after I was done with my scheduled meeting list. My meetings stretched by a half an hour and my lunch was already late. But I knew these adorable kids wouldn't let me go without speaking to them and since I gave them my word, I knew I had to see them, I thought. I called them in. Two boys and three girls.

'Our parents put so much pressure on us,' one of the girls said. 'We want to help other children who go into depression, start taking drugs or become suicidal.'

'That's a great idea,' I said. 'How exactly do you plan on helping them and where do you need my help in making this happen?'

'We need you to speak to the parents and tell them to not pressurize us to always do well in your studies,' the other girl said. 'It's not possible to score well each time.'

'Perhaps, you can write a post,' one of the boys pitched in. 'They need to know that children can't take this pressure.'

'Hmm...' I empathized. 'It's a sad situation. As it is, studies are so boring, I know. On top of that, pressure from parents doesn't help either.'

'Exactly!' another boy concurred. His eyes lit up as he said, 'I wish they also spoke like you.'

'Why do you think they pressurize you to study hard?' I asked them.

'No idea,' they all said. 'Maybe it's good for us but it certainly doesn't feel good. We have no freedom.'

'Do you play any sport?'

'No,' they replied in unison.

'Are you good at anything else like painting, dancing, music or any art form?'

'No,' the two boys said. The girls said they wrote poetry.

'Anyone of you studying at an elite college?'

'No.'

'I suppose each one of you has a phone, maybe a computer, tablet or a laptop too.'

'We all do.'

'And how long do you think your parents should be funding your education or other expenses?' I asked them smilingly.

'Till at least we are out of college.'

'Fair enough,' I said. 'And what after that?'

They told me that, of course, they would take care of their life and expenses themselves. When I asked them what their 'life' entailed, they told me that they would have a nice home, a car or two, sometimes they would go away for vacations without their parents breathing down their necks. They were clear about the kind of gadgets they would have and the life they wanted to lead and how eventually have their own families. They promised me that they would be much better parents, ones who would give their children more freedom.

I'd realized right at the beginning of the conversation that I would have to play the Socrates. No, not by taking on the role of a wise philosopher but as a mere facilitator of a thought process. Socrates was famous for answering a question with another question, making the other person think about what they were saying. Similarly, I just had to help them think through their expectations and assumptions. Hence, I asked them what in their view was needed to make their dreams a reality. To this everyone replied with utmost conviction: money. I lauded their wisdom and further enquired from where that money would come, to which they said, from their earnings. They would, of course, work great jobs that paid them enough so that they could realize their dreams. I reminded them that since none of them was currently studying at or preparing to graduate from the likes of IITs or IIMs, so how would they find a suitable job and what in their opinion the job would pay them. They did not have much information but they posited that they would find a job because they would get a college degree and therefore the salary would easily cover their expenses.

'How much do you think is needed per month to survive in a big city?' I asked.

'Between 8-10,000 rupees per month,' a boy said.

'I think around 15,000 is more realistic,' the other boy said.

'No!' another girl chimed in. 'At least Rs 25,000 is required.'

When I asked them what would be the monthly rent since they would have to take that into consideration, they guessed Rs 10,000 per month. I informed them that with that much money per month in a big city, one usually just about got a room in a shared accommodation. We thought through other expenses like electricity, mobile phone bills, some entertainment, buying clothes, shopping, groceries, commuting expenses and so on. The amount required to sustain even an average lifestyle came to Rs 50,000. That was assuming they didn't have to buy a car, an air-conditioner, etc., and would all be provided by the parents. They would just have to maintain whatever they received.

'And how much do you think you will get per month once you are out of college?'

One boy said, Rs 50,000, the girls said more like 20,000 and the fourth boy said at least 30,000.

'Well, let me tell you something,' I said. 'First of all, the chances of getting a job are not stellar if you graduate from an ordinary college. Secondly, I have known MBAs and MCAs getting Rs 15,000 per month. Recently, the Indian Railways announced 90,000 job openings and there were 25 million candidates who applied. It's almost like you have a better chance at winning a Railway lottery than getting a job.'

Pin-drop silence ensued in the room. I could almost hear them thinking and building towards a conclusion, as if they were arriving at a revelation of sorts. I let them revel in this silence for a good thirty seconds or so. In between, they looked at each other's faces and scanned mine too for any signs of what I might say next.

'So,' I said, 'if you don't play any sports professionally or don't champion any art form, that means you won't be earning anything from a talent or skill. In other words, those who are masters of their skill, may or may not get traditional education, but at least there's some fulfilment by pursuing what matters to them. Apart from this, at a practical level, they have some avenues to generate income by teaching other students. In your case, that option is out. I suppose your only source of income will be from your education. Would that be right to assume, you think?'

They all nodded thoughtfully, but not enthusiastically any more.

'Now we have established you need a minimum of 50,000 rupees per month to live in any metro in India, and that you will earn it from your education, and that with your current education you will be lucky to get a job and even when you do, it won't fetch you more than 15-20,000 per month to begin with. How do you suppose we progress from here?'

They kept quiet for some time before one of the boys said, 'But Steve Jobs and Bill Gates dropped out of college.'

'Good point,' I said. 'They didn't drop out because they found college too hard. They did so because they were already doing something: the expansion and commercialization of their passion in computers. After dropping out, they didn't sit around in pubs, nor did they play video games all night. They didn't just hang out with their friends. They worked hard, very hard.'

'Remember, children,' I continued, 'the amount of money you make in your life is directly proportional to how much value the world places in your offering. If you have something they need, a product, a skill of some kind, they will pay you for it. You need someone to pay you so you may pay your bills.'

'I never thought like that,' the boy said.

'Now, let's come to the end of this discussion,' I said. 'Your parents already know all that I have shared with you. Chances are they may even have told you this many a time in the past. What—'

'No, Swamiji,' one girl cut in hurriedly while the others nodded, 'there's a huge difference in how you've told us and how they did. They don't just tell or ask, they start lecturing. They are just looking for any opportunity to do that. My room is not clean – a big lecture. I am watching TV – a big lecture. I wake up late – a big lecture. I don't go to bed on time – a big lecture. They see me on phone talking to a friend – a big lecture. They never lose an opportunity to rub something in. And—'

'And Swamiji,' one of the boys jumped in, 'every day they tell me how I have everything so easy in my life. Almost every other night at dinner, I have to hear about how they had it very hard when they were growing up. Their parents used to beat them. Well, that's not my fault. Plus, it's not like my father is *Maryada Purushottam* Shri Ram or my mother soft as Sita. You should see when they are fighting, which is just about every other day.'

'That's so true!' the other boy said. 'If I share with them a friend's achievement, I get a big lecture to be like him or her, to follow them. If I bring up how one of my friends is bunking school, smoking cigarettes or failing their classes, I get another big lecture telling me I am not careful in choosing my friends. I just can't have a moment of peace.'

I was really pressed for time and I was hungry too as I was already late for my lunch by more than an hour. But I thought it was important to hear them out.

'What would you do differently if you were in your parents' shoes?' I asked.

'We certainly won't lecture our kids,' they said almost in unison.

'Now, shall I share a method with you so you won't get a lecture from your parents?'

'When I was a child,' I continued, 'I used to ask my parents what was important for them. Good grades and some other house rules, I was told. I promised them that I would get them a good report card and follow house rules (five days in a week) provided they didn't interfere with my day or what I wanted to do in it. At least, once or twice a week, I should be allowed to break some rules and the day I got lower grades at school, I would be happy to surrender my way of life and study and live the way they wanted me to live. Believe me, I was barely in Grade 5 in school when I negotiated that. I lived up to my side of the bargain and scored consistently well and naturally, if they didn't have complaints for me, they had no real reason to lecture me. This way, they were happy that I was being a good boy at school and I was happy because I could pursue things I liked. In other words, learn to negotiate. Don't think that just because they are your parents, they ought to do everything you want in life. You tell me, if you don't study or score well at school, how else are they supposed to say it to you?'

'Swamiji,' one of them said, 'I'm sure I can speak on behalf of everyone here but for the first time in my life, I actually want to study. I realized that if I don't do well in studies, I won't come anywhere close to realizing those dreams.'

'Please know,' I said, 'I'm saying that you've got to do well in something. Whether that's studies, sports, arts, some skill or talent, there's got to be something you master so you may live the life of your dreams. And it's not that if you aren't good at anything, you will die of starvation. It's just that life will be a very ordinary affair for you. The rising price of milk or a rupee increase in the price of petrol, the reality of life will hurt you on a daily basis.'

Seeing how receptive they were, I shared my thoughts on how they could better structure their time to make the most of their lives. Just when I was about to leave, they asked me if I could tell them a joke. This is what I told them:

A family was having their dinner, when the boy said, 'Dad, you think one can eat flies?'

'Eeeew!' the father frowned. 'Don't talk of such gross things while we are having dinner! Eat yours quietly!'

The boy just shrugged and went back to eating his meal.

'Now, what were you asking?' the father said after finishing his meal.

'Don't worry about that question,' the boy replied. 'There was a fly in your salad but that's history now.'

There's no doubt that these kids lent me a better listening ear because I was not their parent. It's somewhat natural for parents, either out of attachment or concern or both, that they want the best for their children. In doing so, sometimes, they overdo everything. Whether that's telling them to just make their bed or turn off their phone, there's a tendency in most parents to overstate things and use way more words than necessary. 'Less is more' is the mantra here.

It is equally important to know that unless we connect with them on an emotional level, we won't be able to get our point across. You must connect before you redirect. Daniel Spilzman, reiterating the findings of neuroscience, states that our left brain represents logic, rationale, linearity, order, etc., whereas the right side of the brain represents feelings, arts, a more holistic approach. He makes a persuasive case in *The Whole-Brain Child* that when they are angry, that's not the time to get their scorecard out and tell them what all they are not doing right.[27] That's the time to connect with the right side of their brain. Logic doesn't connect with emotions. Feelings connect with feelings.

And this brings me to an important point: compassion or empathy. When I say feelings connect with feelings, I'm not suggesting that as a parent you can't be firm with your children or that you are under constant pressure to accede to all their demands or that you always have to handle them with extreme care. On the contrary, it is pivotal to know when to be firm and when to relax. Somewhere, that fine balance is what parenting is all about. Connect before you communicate.

MY THOUGHTS ON…

"... AND THAT SHOULD COVER ALL MY
RULES FOR THE CLASS."

SINGLE PARENTING

I remember how he had entered the classroom with his head hung low. He was extremely sad and none of us knew what to say to him. Even our teacher didn't. Neel was a bright student who was a good soccer player and scored well in class. His family was better off as compared to most of us who belonged to middle-class families for he had the latest video games, a motorbike at the age of thirteen, money to buy drinks and snacks every day at the school canteen and so on. There were two cars in his home and they had plenty of wealth from what he told us or was evident from his lifestyle.

But today he was just standing quietly as he had come to the school after almost one week.

'I'm sorry to hear about your father, Neel,' our teacher said.

He stayed quiet. Just a week ago, his father had a fatal heart attack. He had two more siblings and his father was the sole breadwinner of the family who, despite their wealth, ensured that his children studied hard too. He was the one who ensured discipline at home. His mother was a homemaker. For 99 per cent of other households where only one parent worked, a tragic incident like this would completely break the family. With no government support, no medicare, child support or social security, it would be extremely hard to survive. But in Neel's case, money wasn't the issue. And that ended up being the root cause of him veering off the right path – money wasn't an issue.

Soon, with no one to discipline him and his mother going soft because she didn't want her children to suffer more, Neel's grades dropped. He started to spend more and more of his time on things that didn't matter – from his hairstyle, clothes, video games, cars to girls and everything in between. From a stellar student, he became average and then below-average within six months. The lavishness of his life increased as he became more distant from reality and eventually settled for an ordinary life. For it is a no brainer that if you only keep spending and don't grow your wealth, it will eventually disappear, irrespective of the size of your corpus.

I have met numerous children who were brought up by single parents and they are doing just fine in their lives because any day, being raised by a single parent is certainly better than growing up in a toxic environment where there are frequent fights and arguments. Having said that, I have observed that when parents split and the single parent is able to keep the discipline, the child grows into a stronger and more put together person. If on the other hand, one parent hands a free reign to the child to make up for the absence of the other parent by acceding to their demands and the child ends up much worse. I've also noticed that children of single parents mature faster in their thinking and are better aware of the world. This is based entirely on my observation.

One of the greatest psychologists of modern times, Roy Bumeister, cites an interesting study by Walter Mischel, presenting a correlation between the willpower of children and single parents.

Before his famous marshmallow experiments (covered in the chapter – Delayed Gratification) with children near Stanford University, Walter Mischel made another discovery about self-control while working in Trinidad. He went there with the intention of studying ethnic stereotypes. The two main ethnic groups in rural Trinidad were of different descent, one African, the other Indian, and they held negative but different stereotypes of each other. The Indians regarded the Africans as lacking in future orientation and inclined to indulge rather than save, whereas the Africans regarded the Indians as joyless savers who lacked a zest for life. Mischel decided to test these stereotypes by asking children from each group to choose between two candy bars. One candy bar was bigger and cost ten times as much as the other, but a child who chose it would have to wait a week to get it. The smaller, cheaper one was available right away.

Mischel found some support for the ethnic stereotypes, but in the process he stumbled on a much bigger and more meaningful effect. Children who had a father in the home were far more willing than others

*to choose the delayed reward. Most of the racial and
ethnic variation could be explained by this difference
because the Indian children generally lived with both
parents, whereas a fair number of the African children
lived with a single mother. The value of fatherhood was
also evident when Mischel analyzed just the African
homes: about half of the children living with fathers
chose the delayed reward, but none of the children in
fatherless homes were willing to wait. Similarly, none of
the Indian children living without a father were willing
to wait.*[28]

In fact, there's a very strong correlation between
monitoring your child and how well those children do in
their lives. Many studies have found that when children
are monitored, especially during their teen years, they
are more together, functional and successful later in their
lives. By monitoring, I don't mean you subject them to
surveillance but knowing what your child is up to when
not at home, who they are hanging out with, how they are
doing in school, can make a huge difference to the choices
they make in life. Parents who, in the name of freedom or
trust, keep themselves away from their children's life and
choices are in a way doing a great disservice to themselves
and their offspring.

Often, the kind of conversations children witness at
home are the ones they hold when they grow up. If at
home, the environment is negative with one or both
parents often complaining and whining, they pass this
on to their children as well. I read somewhere that small
minds discuss people, average minds discuss events

while great minds discuss ideas. They will only do what they see.

It also pays to remember that you can only be mindful and do the best you can. There is no set right or wrong when it comes to parenting. There can't be, for every parent and every child is unique. Even for a moment, I'm not suggesting that you should stay on in an abusive relationship just because you want to provide a two-parent home for your children. What is infinitely more important is to build a culture of resilience and responsibility at home.

In my meeting hundreds of children face to face, I've observed that young and neo adults who are lazy and lead an irresponsible life are the first ones to blame everything on their parents or childhood. In a functional family of, let's say, four siblings, if two are successful or generally positive, I never hear from them that their parents messed up their lives. The other two, who might be struggling in their careers or relationships, are quick to conclude that their parents let them down.

Many children brought up by single parents say they failed because their parents couldn't stay together. For parents who do stay together, kids complain that the parents argue and fight and it would be better if they were separated. To the soft parents, they say that they are not firm or strong enough to make important decisions for them. To the parents who are there for their children, they tell me that their parents are forever watching them and telling them what to do. To the parents who gave freedom to their children, the kids say that their parents just didn't watch out for them, they didn't protect them.

Every parent has been an unwilling player in the you-can't-win game. Require your daughter to take piano lessons, and later she will complain that you wrecked her love of the piano. Let your daughter give up lessons because she didn't want to practise, and later she will complain that you should have forced her to keep going — why, now she can't play the piano at all. Require your son to go to Hebrew school in the afternoon, and he will blame you for having kept him from becoming another Hank Greenberg. Allow your son to skip Hebrew school, and he will later blame you for his not feeling more connected to his heritage. Betsy Petersen produced a full-bodied whine in her memoir, Dancing with Daddy, *blaming her parents for only giving her swimming lessons, trampoline lessons, horseback-riding lessons, and tennis lessons, but not ballet lessons. 'The only thing I wanted, they would not give me,' she wrote. Parent blaming is a popular and convenient form of self-justification because it allows people to live less uncomfortably with their regrets and imperfections.*[29]

If your kids say you are responsible for everything that isn't going right in their lives, it doesn't mean you are a bad parent. It means they are trying to fill a void, not by understanding what they can do to better their lives but by shifting the responsibility of their own choices and actions onto you. It's about time you freed yourself from the resentment, regret or the guilt. And if you truly believe you made some terrible mistakes – not because of what your children are saying but based on what you know – then, apologize and move on because we can't undo the past. Even if you made a mistake, it doesn't mean everything undesirable in their lives is the result of that. Besides, what your child thinks may not necessarily be what's true. In psychology, it is called cognitive dissonance, meaning a way of self-justification. The only thing to bear in mind is that children will do what they see you doing and not what you ask them to do.

I remember when we were growing up, the iron-clad rule at home was that the TV would be turned off by 9 p.m. Only on Saturdays, were we allowed to watch till 10.30 p.m. When my sister crossed the age of eighteen (which means my brother was fifteen and I was twelve back then), she loved watching two programmes on TV. One was called *Oshin*, a Japanese show about the story of a woman who made it from rags to riches and another one called *Byomkesh Bakshi*. Our father made an exception and we were allowed to watch it with her. But here's the important thing: he would turn off the TV at 9 p.m. himself. Since the TV was off and no one else in the family was watching it, it didn't require an enormous willpower to stay away from it. We were required to do some reading and then go to bed. When you do the things you want your kids to do, eventually they'll start doing it. A little anecdote here:

Some guests arrived home for a dinner. At the table, a mother turned to her six-year-old and said, 'Would you like to say grace?'

'But I don't know what to say!'

'Just say whatever I say,' the mother said. 'Oh, God! Why on earth have I invited these people to dinner?' Innocently spoke the little girl.

Whether you are a single parent or not, the only way to have your children live a certain way is to live that way yourself and with utmost sincerity. If they see you happy doing the things you do, they'll automatically be attracted to your ways. They will follow the actions you rejoice in doing.

THINGS THAT MATTER

Ithought about ending this book on a philosophical note, something like a nice dessert that leaves a good taste in your mouth. But then I figured that I must sum up this book with some practical tips or what I think are more practical tips. After all, after every meal you eat out, you do receive a bill. This chapter is something like that: a gentle reminder of what we covered in the book with some things we didn't cover. It's like getting a dessert on the house or those candies with your bill. Here are the ten golden rules – I mean tentative guidelines, of parenting.

1. Say Yes More Than You Say No

'As a species, we are more compelled to avoid pain than to seek out pleasure. This is why studies have shown that we are hurt more by losing \$5,000 than by we are pleased by winning \$5,000,' says Tim David.[30] On most occasions, parents want their children to behave like adults even when they are just three or four years old. Most certainly, children should be taught manners, etiquette and civility from an early age but that does not mean our default response to everything they ask for or say is 'no'. You will be surprised by how common it is for a parent's first answer to almost every request to be a 'no' before they'll consider saying 'yes'. This eventually results in a child's brain to filter out a 'no' as noise. Say 'yes' more. It won't hurt you.

2. Admit When You Are at Fault

For children, parents are their role models – certainly early on in their lives. If you make a mistake, simply go up to your children and say sorry, you were wrong. It'll go a long way in strengthening your relationship with your child. Plus, you'll earn their respect and they will learn to trust you more. If they ask you a question and you don't know the answer, simply say, 'I don't know, let's find out together!' rather than making up an answer and passing it on. The more they see you as real, the more they'll relate to you, thus leading to a better connection. And an emotional connection is the first requirement if you want them to listen to you.

3. Respect Each Other and Keep Your Arguments in the Bedroom

If two partners don't respect each other, you can be almost certain that your children won't respect you or their siblings. There's absolutely no doubt that making a marriage work can be a tiring affair at times and a bond as intimate as marriage, disagreements and conflicts are natural. But, in many households, parents expect their children to behave like adults while they themselves behave like kids. No matter how grave the disagreement, make it a point (I know it is easier said than done, but at least you are aware), to talk about it in your bedroom. When was the last time you resolved any issue by arguing or shouting? Just steadily work on building that mindfulness so you can act in a responsible manner in the face of stress and conflict. Your children are going to imitate your response.

4. Channelize their Energy

Children are bursting with energy and if you are not going to help them harness and channelize it, it would take the form of anger, aggression or maybe even plain laziness. If there's one thing I recommend the most, it would be to introduce them to a physical activity like a sport or a creative activity like arts and music early on in their lives. This will help them pick themselves up and move on when life knocks them down. And when they may be down, they will have something to hold on to. Here's what I mean by channelizing their energy:

Introduce Them to Playing a Sport

When they are very young, let them get on the field or a court rather than a street. Playing physical sports encourages sharing, teamwork, positive competition and above all channels their energy into the right place. Not to mention it's great for health. You may take them to swimming, tennis, badminton, etc., and after a year or so they may show an inclination towards only one particular sport. Help them pursue it. If it's something even parents play, children are a lot more likely to follow. Almost all athletes who turn pros start at a very early age, sometimes as young as three years old.

Introduce a Creative Activity

Of all the people I meet, the ones lost are those who have no passion in life. Introducing your child to a mental activity like chess or a creative one like painting, drawing, playing a musical instrument or singing and so on will tremendously help them in life. Creative people do get depressed or sad too. But when they do, they are able to turn inwards and draw energy from their talents. The notion of passion is best introduced early on. Those who have one passion find it natural to shift their energy to another. You will be doing your children a great service by putting them in some creative activity. Just remember that for both creative and physical activity they will need to be nudged gently in the beginning. Once they taste the joy a bit, they would want to do nothing else but turn their hobby into their life's purpose.

Build the Habit of Reading

Children who read while growing up become more mature thinkers in life. They are more together, less rigid and are more open to possibilities and perspectives in life.

They may start with story books and gradually move on to good literature. It's pivotal that they read good books but not the kind that'll incite them. Having said that, they would want to read all kinds of books and you can't stop them and it's okay to read all kinds of books but begin with good books. People in the habit of reading are not as easily bored compared to those who don't.

Hear Them Out

Allow children to express themselves freely without any fear. Sometimes, all they are looking for is someone to listen to them. They don't always need advice. Resist that urge – it can break down communication very fast. If you want to be interesting for them – so they want to know what you have to say – you must be interested in them first. In other words, be interested before you become interesting.

5. Encourage Action Not Outcome

From the perspective of behavioural science, one thing is very clear: any behaviour you accept will be encouraged. And any behaviour you encourage will repeat itself. When you praise your child for an outcome, all it does is create pressure on them to somehow repeat the outcome. It takes away the joy of attainment. It is more powerful to instead praise their effort and be specific about which particular act of theirs you found noteworthy. Don't shower excessive praise, it loses its value. Many studies have confirmed it and it has also been my personal observation after speaking to numerous children that they try really hard to impress their parents. They want to please you and make you proud. It may seem the contrary, but it's the truth.

6. Let Them Sleep

If you wake up early and you think that your children should do the same, you are not being reasonable. Biological sleep patterns shift while growing up, especially in teenagers. It is perfectly normal for them to not go to sleep till 11 p.m. and to wake up late. Their brain is wired that way. Teenagers need an average of eight to ten hours of sleep every night and children who sleep well are less prone to depression, anxiety and many other disorders. As they age, their sleep patterns will change automatically, particularly in healthy adults, and will lean towards going to bed early and waking up early. In other words, don't worry, give it time and they'll become like you.

7. Be Reasonable

Sometimes out of attachment, love or confidence, we begin to expect too much from children. A good parent knows that not everyone can achieve everything. Some kids are naturally better at some things than others. It's not fair to try and fulfil our dreams through our children. Be reasonable, be real.

I once heard a famous pianist talk about teaching his students. 'I don't believe in teaching them what they should be learning,' he said. 'My job is to help them so they get in touch with themselves. The rest is easy. Because then they know exactly what they want and what it is that they are good at and I just join them on their journey.' Sometimes we overload children with unreasonable expectations around behaviour, morality, discipline and so on. At that moment, just take a deep breath and ask yourself most honestly, 'What was I doing when I was his age?'

8. Introduce Spirituality

Before I say anything further, I must specify that by saying 'introduce spirituality', I'm not saying 'make them fanatics'. I've seen that children brought up in spiritual, even religious, environments have one more anchor in life. When parents, siblings, friends and family are not around to spend time or help, faith in God can do miracles to one's state of mind. The golden rule, however, is to not push too hard. If they can do a five-minute prayer in the morning or evening and they can say grace before they eat, that's good enough. Do remember that when they are children, they may say their prayers and so on. Towards their teenage years, they may rebel completely and stop praying altogether. They may even tell you that they don't believe in God. Don't panic, don't react. Let them grow through that phase. In their early twenties, they'll be busy with their ambition, careers and sexual freedom. Once they settle down a bit more in life, say, when they reach their thirties, they'll come back to the same values they learnt when they were children; provided you didn't force them to practise religion at the time. If you did, they are most likely to turn complete atheists. Multiple studies have shown that children who are encouraged to practise spirituality, whether in the form of prayers or meditation, have better control over themselves.

9. Tell Them the Truth

Children are lot more resilient than we think they are. And one definitive way to make them stronger and even more resilient is to tell them the truth. If you are sincere and truthful about your own life and feelings, their love and respect for you will grow multifold. Be gentle and speak softly when you share your feelings with them, keeping in mind that the idea is not to make them realize they can't help you or that they have hurt you. The idea is that you want to share how *you* are feeling and not necessarily what others have made you feel. It doesn't matter how beautiful a lie may be, ultimately truth alone prevails. It'll keep them real.

10. Keep It Light

Don't make life such a serious affair. Remember the P of parenting: to make things playful. Maybe you are certain about what they should be doing in life but that may not be the only way. Keep up the playfulness and joy in life. It's a short one. And ultimately, everything is impermanent and cyclical. Everyone is here with a role to play; you must play yours and let them play theirs.

Please resist the temptation to take this book to your child and say, 'See, read here! I've been telling you all this all along and you don't listen to me.' If you must share it with them, just say, 'Wow! I read this book that shows where I've been going wrong as a parent. So many things

I didn't know.' This may make them want to read it. If you want them to follow someone, refrain from asking them to follow that person or ceaselessly talking about your role model. They will start to hate that person before even meeting him or her. Instead, just gently mention the name here and there, drop in a line or two, keep it real by sometimes being critical of your role model and then wait and watch. It'll happen. They'll come around.

Every child is born with a certain predisposition, proclivities and tendencies. A parent can only help children get in touch with themselves, nature then takes its own course.

There's nothing called an extraordinary child, only an extraordinary childhood. Good parenting is what makes it extraordinary.

LIST OF ILLUSTRATIONS

These illustrations have been sourced under publishing license from cartoonstock.com.

NOTES

1   Wikipedia: wikipedia.org/wiki/László_Polgár; Last accessed on 6 February 2019.

2   You can read the full article here: independent.co.uk/lifestyle/a-man-with-a-talent-for-creating-genius-william-hartston-meets-laszlo-polgar-the-father-of-three-1478062.html; *Independent*; Last accessed on 6 February 2019.

3   The line 'Every child is a promise' has been taken from the book by Laszlo. The whole story of how Laszlo and Klara Polgar raised their children, in an interview format, is covered in *Nevelj zsenit*! It was translated from Hungarian into English by Gordon Tisher as *Raise a Genius!* The book is available for a free reading or download on scribd: scribd.com/document/365769004/Raise-a-Genius-Polgar

4   You can read more on Hygge in *The Little Book of Hygge: The Danish Way to Live Well* by Meik Wiking. In short, Hygge is the Danish concept of togetherness. It may mean friends getting together and sipping hot coffee or chocolate in a cozy room next to a fireplace when it's snowing outside or it could mean just feeling very warm inside in good company. It's a beautiful way of life, that some contend, is at the root of Danish happiness. One of my most favourite quotes in the

book read: 'We are not paying taxes. We are investing in a society. We are purchasing quality of life.'

5   *The Danish Way of Parenting: What the Happiest People in the World Know About Raising Confident, Capable Kids* by Jessica Joelle Alexander and Iben Dissing Sandahl; published in December 2014. The book cites four styles of parenting.

> *Authoritarian: These parents are demanding and not responsive. They want obedience and have high standards – the classic tiger mom. Children of authoritarian parents tend to do well in school but sometimes suffer from low self-esteem, depression and poor social skills.*
>
> *Authoritative (not to be confused with authoritarian): These parents are demanding but responsive. They set high standards as well but are supportive in their discipline. Children of authoritative parents are rated more socially and intellectually competent than those of other parents.*
>
> *Permissive: These parents are highly responsive but seldom demand mature behaviour from their child, depending instead on self-regulation from the child. Children of permissive parents tend to have problems in school and with their behaviour in general.*
>
> *Uninvolved: These parents are neither responsive nor demanding, but not to the point of being neglectful. Children of uninvolved parents do most poorly in all areas.*

6   Ibid.

7   You can read the whole article by William Doyle on smh. com.au/national/this-is-why-finland-has-the-best-schools-20160325-gnqv9l.html; Last accessed on 6 February 2019. One particular paragraph that struck a deep chord with me was: *'Our mission as adults is to protect our children from politicians,'* one Finnish childhood education professor told me. *'We also have an ethical and moral responsibility to tell businesspeople to stay out of our building.' In fact, any Finnish citizen is free to visit any school whenever they like, but her message was clear: Educators*

are the ultimate authorities on education, not bureaucrats, and not technology vendors.

I wish we had a vision of a better school system in India too where we focused on nurturing our children rather than getting caught up in the mess of politics, bureaucracy, caste and religion.

If you wish to read more about the Finnish way of schooling, I encourage you to read this wonderful article *Why Are Finland's Schools Successful?* by Lynnell Hancock on smithsonianmag.com/innovation/why-are-finlands-schools-successful-49859555/; Last accessed on 6 February 2019.

8   *The Danish Way of Parenting: What the Happiest People in the World Know About Raising Confident, Capable Kids* by Jessica Joelle Alexander, et al; published in December 2014.

9   Ibid.

10 Ibid.

11 Ibid.

12 Ibid.

13 You can read the full article here: cmu.edu/news/stories/archives/2014/december/december17_hugsprotect.html; Last accessed on 6 February 2019.

14 Taken from *Let Me Tell You A Story* by Tony Campolo.

15 The study I'm referring to was done by Feldman et al in 2000 at MIT. If you wish to read in more detail, I encourage you to pick up a book he published ten years later: *The Liar in Your Life: The Way to Truthful Relationships* by Robert Feldman, published in August 2009.

16 In *Nurtureshock: Why Everything We Thought About Children Is Wrong*, published in January 2011, the authors visit Dr Victoria Talwar. They are shown eight videos of children telling a story when they were bullied. They had to guess if the child in the video was telling the truth or narrating a completely fabricated story. The children (aged between seven and eleven) in the experiment were coached briefly the night before. Out of the eight stories, one author could

only guess four right and the other only three. When police officers are asked to guess, they get it right only 45 per cent of the time. When teachers take the same test, usually they get 60 per cent right. This book has other interesting and fabulous insights on upbringing of children.

17 *No-Drama Discipline: The Whole-Brain Way to Calm the Chaos and Nurture Your Child's Developing Mind (Mindful Parenting)* by Daniel J. Siegel and Tina Payne Bryson, published in July 2016. This book offers some interesting insights into how so often a child's reactions are not in her control because her brain is changing. The regions of the brain that govern understanding and emotional response are still developing when they are growing up. A good read, overall.

18 Oscar Wilde, *The Importance of Being Earnest*.

19 I heard it in the lectures of Alan Watts called *Out of Mind* (Audible book). There's a particular talk called *The Web of Life*, and within it: *What Game Would You Like To Play?* is where he talked about it.

20 I highly recommend reading *The Defining Decade: Why Your Twenties Matter and How to Make the Most of Them Now* by Meg Jay, a clinical psychologist. Many young adults (and parents too) will benefit much from this read.

21 You can find a more detailed biography of Erik Erikson on his Wikipedia page: wikipedia.org/wiki/Erik_Erikson. Or if you wish to read some of his works then *Identity and the Life Cycle* and *Childhood And Society* are not bad either. Please note, however, that these works read quite academic and you can clearly see Sigmund Freud's influence in Erik's theses. And, admittedly, at 400+ pages, I couldn't go through *Childhood and Society* in its entirety. Another book, *The Life Cycle Completed* which he co-authored with his wife, Joan Erikson, is more readable. Some of his writings are still relevant, most notably the eight stages of psychological crisis though I don't quite agree with the clear demarcation of stages and ages as stated by Erikson. In case you are interested, here they are:

Stage	Psychosocial Crisis	Basic Virtue	Age
1.	Trust vs Mistrust	Hope	0 - 1½
2.	Autonomy vs Shame	Will	1½ - 3
3.	Initiative vs Guilt	Purpose	3 - 5
4.	Industry vs Inferiority	Competency	5 - 12
5.	Identity vs Role Confusion	Fidelity	12 - 18
6.	Intimacy vs Isolation	Love	18 - 40
7.	Generativity vs Stagnation	Care	40 - 65
8.	Ego Integrity vs Despair	Wisdom	65+

To know a summary of what each of these stages mean, you can read *Erik Erikson* on SimplyPsychology.com (the table above has been taken from this website). Available at simplypsychology.org/Erik-Erikson.html; Last accessed on 6 February 2019.

22 You can read more on this in Adam Alter's wonderful book, *Irresistible: The Rise of Addictive Technology and the Business of Keeping Us Hooked.*

23 *Willpower: Rediscovering Our Greatest Strength by Roy F. Baumeister and John Tierney*

24 Many years ago, I read the wonderful book *Flow: The Psychology of Optimal Experience* by Mihaly Csikszentmihalyi. It is a slow read, quite academic in prose, but with some great insights. The one thing this book reminded me was how 'flow' in Mihaly's work was so similar to the concept of samadhi in Vedic texts. Mihaly spent twenty-five years in researching the phenomenon called Happiness. Here's something beautiful he has to say:

What I 'discovered' was that happiness is not something that happens. It is not the result of good fortune or random chance. It is not something that money can buy or power command. It does not depend on outside events, but, rather, on how we interpret them. Happiness, in fact, is a condition that must be prepared for, cultivated, and defended privately by each person. People who learn to control inner experience will be able to determine the quality of their lives, which is as close as any of us can come to being happy.

Yet we cannot reach happiness by consciously searching for it. 'Ask yourself whether you are happy,' said J.S. Mill, 'and you cease to be so.' It is by being fully involved with every detail of our lives, whether good or bad, that we find happiness, not by trying to look for it directly. Viktor Fankl, the Austrian psychologist, summarized it beautifully in the preface to his book Man's Search for Meaning: 'Don't aim at success — the more you aim at it and make it a target, the more you are going to miss it. For success, like happiness, cannot be pursued; it must ensue … as the unintended side-effect of one's personal dedication to a course greater than oneself.'

25 I took the Pali translation by Thannisaro Bhikku. You can find it in Abhaya Sutta (Manjhim Nikaya, 58) on accesstoinsight.org/tipitaka/mn/mn.058.than.html; Last accessed on 7 February 2019.

26 Dan opens the first chapter 'Paying More for Less' with a description of the mouse, maze and the experiment I cite in my chapter. As follows:

Imagine that you are a plump, happy laboratory rat. One day, a gloved human hand carefully picks you out of the comfy box you call home and places you into a different, less comfy box that contains a maze. Since you are naturally curious, you begin to wander around, whiskers twitching along the way. You quickly notice that some parts of the maze are black and others are white. You follow your nose into a white section. Nothing happens. Then you take a left turn into a black section. As soon as you enter, you feel a very nasty shock surge through your paws.

> *Every day for a week, you are placed in a different maze. The dangerous and safe places change daily, as do the colours of the walls and the strength of the shocks. Sometimes the sections that deliver a mild shock are coloured red. Other times, the parts that deliver a particularly nasty shock are marked by polka dots. Sometimes the safe parts are covered with black-and-white checks. Each day, your job is to learn to navigate the maze by choosing the safest paths and avoiding the shocks (your reward for learning how to safely navigate the maze is that you aren't shocked).*

The Upside of Irrationality: The Unexpected Benefits of Defying Logic at Work and at Home (published in May 2011) is full of interesting case studies and makes for a good read as is Dan Airely's earlier book, *Predictably Irrational: The Hidden Forces That Shape Our Decisions* (published in April 2010), which shows however rational or logical we may think, our decisions are, in reality though, anything about rational. In the context of parenting too, this book shows why we can't use logic to help our children when emotions take them over.

27   *The Whole-Brain Child: 12 Revolutionary Strategies to Nurture Your Child's Developing Mind* by Daniel J. Siegel and Tina Payne Bryson is a good book on parenting. Some parts of it are very nice. Well researched and scientific in its approach, it offers good food for thought. Published in September 2012.

28   Taken from *Willpower: Rediscovering Our Greatest Strength* by Roy F. Baumeister and John Tierney (published in October 2011). While the book is not on parenting, it's full of fascinating studies offering great insights on human behaviour and, as the name says, strengthening your willpower. On the topic of parenting, Baumeister contends in the book that children brought up by both parents get better grades in school. It is important to point out here that single parent out of choice (divorce, separation or estrangement) is not the same

as a single parent out of circumstances (job requirements, widowhood, etc.). While searching for an explanation on why children in two-parent homes are healthier and better-adjusted emotionally, he goes on to say:

> *One possible explanation is that children in one-parent homes start off with a genetic disadvantage in self-control. After all, if the father (or mother, for that matter) has run off and abandoned the family, he may have genes favouring impulsive behaviour and undermining self-control, and his children might have inherited those same genes. Some researchers have attempted to correct for this by looking at children who were raised by single parents because the father was absent for reasons other than having abandoned the family (like being stationed overseas for a long time, or dying at a young age). Predictably, the results were in between. These children showed some deficits, but their problems were not as large as those of the children whose fathers had voluntarily left the home. The evidence suggested that, as usual, children are shaped by a mixture of genetics and the environment.*
>
> *Whatever role is played by genes, there's an obvious environmental factor affecting children in single-parent homes: they're being watched by fewer eyes. Monitoring is a crucial aspect of self-control, and two parents can generally do a better job of monitoring. Single parents are so busy with essential tasks – putting food on the table, keeping the child healthy, paying bills – that they have to put a lower priority on making and enforcing rules. Two parents can divide the work, leaving them both with more time and energy to spend building the child's character.*

29   *Mistakes were Made (But Not by Me)* by Carol Tavris and Elliot Aronson. It's a great book to read if you want to know how we can sometimes be blind to our own choices and justify everything that we do. Published in October 2015.

30 Tim David expounds on the psychology of personal and interpersonal communication with what he calls 'Magic Words' in his concise book: *Magic Words: The Science and Secrets Behind Seven Words that Motivate, Engage, and Influence* (published in December 2014). I thought the book was a lovely read and encourage you to read it to understand how to communicate more effectively. Just for your reference, the seven magic words in his book are: 1. Yes, 2. But, 3. Because, 4. Their Name, 5. If, 6. Help and 7. Thanks.